Around the World in Forty-Five Years

My Memorable Career with the Department of Defense Overseas Schools

Thomas Ellinger

Around the World in Forty-Five Years
My Memorable Career with the Department of Defense Overseas Schools

First Edition: 2020

ISBN: 9781524315764
ISBN eBook: 9781524315863

For My Daughter Kathryn
and Grandsons, Ben and Max

Acknowledgments

To my mother, who physically insured my survival during WWII and who saved my weekly letters home, which were used as a basis for this work,

To my wife Liz, who followed me around the globe, generously lending support and encouragement,

To my mentors, who believed in me and who allowed me to serve in a variety of educational positions,

To our brave men and women in uniform, our parents and commanders, who generously supported our schools' mission,

To the committed DoDDS teachers, administrators, and district staff with whom I was privileged to serve, including Anita Dragoo for her professional editing and helpful suggestions in expanding the manuscript,

Thank you!

Prologue

I have always had a fascination for geography and travel. In my early years, living in Germany during World War II, I taught an imaginary world geography class from a map which I pinned up on a wall in our house. My seventh-grade geography teacher in Cincinnati, Ms. Olga Sinning, made this subject come alive in her class, and from then on, I wanted to be a teacher and to travel.

When, in the winter of 1960, a fabulous opportunity printed in the *Cincinnati Enquirer* came to my attention, "Teach Overseas and See the World," I did not hesitate to leave home and travel 13,000 miles by train and ship to my first overseas assignment in the exotic Far East.

Subsequent assignments as a teacher, counselor, elementary, junior, and senior high school principal, and superintendent in Germany, Korea, and the Mediterranean District, which included Turkey, Spain, Bahrain, the Azores, and Italy, rounded out a fabulous career of forty-five years in education. In addition to my career assignments, I had the opportunity to travel to seventy plus countries across Asia, Europe, Africa, Central and South America.

Throughout this book, I refer to the acronym **DoDDS** which stands for *Department of Defense Dependent Schools*, the worldwide school system of which I was a part and which continues to serve the children of our Armed Forces men and women and Department of Defense Civilian employees in 12 countries.

Although parts of this book may sound like a travelogue, I believe that I was focused on our school's principal mission, to provide a top-quality education to the students of our brave military men and women serving overseas. I had the distinct privilege to meet outstanding military enlisted and officer personnel who were our parents and commanders and who insured that our schools' mission received top billing while their spouses contributed countless hours to PTA, School Advisory Councils, Booster Clubs, Scholarship Award Committees, and other school activities.

It was rewarding to work with our resilient students who frequently moved from school to school and country to country, leaving their friends behind, only to start again the process of settling in.

Finally, I had the good fortune to interact personally with hundreds of dedicated Department of Defense teachers, administrators, and district personnel whose professionalism always exceeded my expectations.

[1]

Bombs over Frankfurt

I was born in Frankfurt, Germany on February 20,1935, just a few years after Adolf Hitler and his Nazi Party seized power and established their police state. I recall little of my early childhood except that my father left home. However, I have been told that because he was Jewish, Dad was interned for a time in Buchenwald, a concentration camp near Weimar, until his bosses at the *Metallgesellschaft*, a Frankfurt firm vital in the war effort, in cooperation with an American Quaker group, miraculously gained his release. I was only three when he was allowed to depart in 1938, first for England, then later to the United States in search of a job, and I would not see him again until I was almost twelve.

My mother and father were only authorized to correspond through the Swiss Red Cross in a censored letter limited to just thirty words, which took three months to arrive in either Germany or the States. Dad was finally able to send ship tickets in 1941. However, by that time, Japan had bombed Pearl Harbor in Hawaii and the United States had joined the war against both Japan and Hitler. My mother, brother Steve, and I had no choice but to remain in Germany.

My mother tells me that on my first day of school in 1939, she and others lined up with their children at the front of the elementary building for all- male students. The principal told them, "You are entrusting your sons to the *Führer*, Adolf Hitler, in the service of the *Vaterland*."

Teachers were required to belong to the Nazi party to keep their jobs. My first-grade teacher, *Herr* Debus, was a strict but kind gentleman. He sometimes used his hickory stick to strike students across the hand if we were unruly, too slow to say the times tables, exhibited poor handwriting, or failed to bring in homework. We learned to dread having the principal interrupt our lessons to take students out of class, for he usually was there to inform them of the serious injury or death of their fathers in the war effort. In class, we eagerly followed Rommel's early battles and victories in the Africa campaign, envisioning his panzer tanks rolling through the desert. We listened on the radio to Hitler's speeches, and we marched to patriotic songs on the playground, taking turns carrying the blood red swastika flag in front of the class.

Frankfurt was spared during the early war years because the Allies, Britain and the United States, announced they would make the city their headquarters at the conclusion of hostilities. Consequently, life for my family continued rather peacefully, although our father was absent. We lived in a comfortable apartment of a three-family row house in Sachsenhausen, a suburb of Frankfurt on the south side of the Main River, and, as far as I knew, we had plenty to eat. As a boy of eight, I had little concept then of the horrors of war. When I was in the third grade, I started a small diary which began with this initial entry:

> *Erntedankfest*, German Thanksgiving. My mother, brother, grandmother and I went on a typical Sunday stroll to *Oberrad*, relishing the colorful fall foliage in the Sachsenhausen woods. We visited the local church where the altar was laden with apples, pears, plums, and vegetables, a grateful reminder of a bountiful

harvest and a good year. We stopped for coffee and cake on the way back to our home.

The following day, October 3, 1943, was a day that would be etched into my memory for the rest of my life.

As usual, I trekked to my third-grade class in the Gellert School, a good four miles into the city. When the air-raid siren sounded in mid-morning to signal the approach of enemy aircraft, we thought, this is just another drill. Nevertheless, all of us children and teachers made our way down what seemed like hundreds of stairs to the underground shelter. Suddenly, we heard the shrill whistling of bombs streaking through the air, followed by deafening explosions as they hit their targets. Some children began screaming and sobbing hysterically, and the teachers quickly ushered them out to an isolated room. After some anxious waiting, we heard the sirens sounding the "all clear" and we were dismissed from school. I can still recall the crimson clouds and pillars of black smoke rising into the autumn sky as I made the long uphill hike to my family's home in Sachsenhausen.

That same evening shortly after nine, Steve and I were barely in bed when the sirens sounded again. Our basement shelter, which had connecting doors between our neighbors' cellars and ours, had been fortified with additional beams by a crew of Italian workers during the summer. I snatched up a book and followed my brother and mother down the stairs.

I tried to concentrate on my reading as we sat for an hour in eerie silence. Against all hope, we heard the distant roar of approaching planes, followed by anti-aircraft fire, and then the whistle and impact of incendiary bombs. A loud crash signaled that our neighbor's house on the left was struck, and this family soon joined us in our shelter. Immediately following the impact, the lights went out, while splinters of furniture, glass, and personal belongings rained down the cellar steps. Smelling the fumes from the burning house, my mother wrapped Steve and me in wet sheets, hoping this would prevent our clothes from catching fire.

After the planes had left, we climbed up the stairs and out the door into a glowing inferno. The streets were literally on fire due to the phosphorous bombs that had been dropped. All of us neighborhood children were herded into the basement of the only apartment complex left untouched by the air raid while our mothers and a few retired men were ordered by police to go to the top of the flat roof and assist with extinguishing sparks and flames from the surrounding buildings. Much later, my family and I were invited by friends into their apartment and spent the remainder of the night in a fitful and exhausted sleep.

Unfortunately, the neighboring city of Mainz had suffered a huge air raid the previous evening and most of the fire equipment available in the Frankfurt area had been taken there. So, when we assessed our damage, it was much greater than it would have been had Frankfurt had the necessary resources. We discovered that a large bomb had hit our house after our exit, leaving only one wall and the chimney intact, with part of our grand piano dangling precariously from the top of the chimney.

A van with a loudspeaker went through the streets, announcing that all the homeless should report to the *Hauptbahnhof*—main railroad station—that evening in order to be housed temporarily in surrounding towns and villages. Mom, Steve, and I returned to our place with a small cart and were able to save a few undamaged boxes from our basement, mainly clothes and a set of china. When we finished, we went into a small restaurant nearby where we could get slices of bread with marmalade and coffee. Later that afternoon, we and our neighbors joined a long procession of refugees trudging out of Sachsenhausen, across the Main River, and through the partially demolished Altstadt, the old town of Frankfurt, to the main train station.

Our designated train stood ready on Track Five, but just before its departure, the air raid sirens pierced the air and they herded us into the station's bomb shelter. Again, we waited, trembling, for the whining whistle of approaching bombs. But this time, there was no direct hit on Frankfurt, and after two hours, the train was able to depart.

All homeowners in the vicinity of large cities had been asked to prepare a number of rooms for victims of the air raids. The train stopped at various stations along the route, names were called, and families disembarked to go to their temporary homes. We were told to leave the train at the little Taunus mountain town of Bad Soden northwest of Frankfurt, a place well known for sulfur springs and treatment of heart patients. My mother, brother, and I followed our escort to the home of a local family who welcomed us as new boarders.

I completed my third year of school while living with the Von Scheven family and their two sons. Although Bad Soden was a relatively quiet town, it was near the Frankfurt suburb of Hoechst, one of the centers of the German chemical industry and thus important to the war effort. Not surprisingly, Hoechst became a frequent target of Allied raids, and we often saw the crimson sky from our window early in the morning.

My mother, brother, grandmother, and I eventually moved to the small village of Steinbach, a rustic village in the *Westerwald* area where we rented a couple of rooms in a local farmhouse. For a while, the huge barn connected to the house was occupied by Russian prisoners of war who were allowed to work on neighboring farms during the day, then returned to our place in the evening. Since she spoke a little Russian, my grandmother befriended the soldiers—farmers from Siberia, who, like all fathers, were proud to show us photos of their families back home.

In Steinbach, Steve and I attended a local two- room schoolhouse. Grades one through four were taught by *Frau* Schmidt, and grades five through eight by *Herr* Schmidt. Although the instruction was traditional, we were afforded a good solid education in the basics.

At the rear of the room, we students took turns monitoring the radio, listening for announcements that Allied planes had crossed the German border. Immediately, our teachers dismissed us from school. During my fifth-grade year, as the raids on neighboring larger towns became daily occurrences, formal instruction ceased. Each evening at dusk, a town announcer reported the national news from various strategic places in the village. As far as Germany's position in the war was concerned, the news was always positive. It didn't matter how many towns were bombed or whether there were tragic defeats at the Western Front or in Stalingrad. Goebbel's propaganda machine did its best to keep the masses ignorant. Listening to foreign news reports on shortwave radio was punishable with prison. At the end of the evening newscast, the village announcer would read an order by the mayor directing students to report to school the following day to work in support of the war effort. We gathered wood, debugged potato plants, and picked berries and mushrooms, among other chores. While the farmers always had food to eat, most of us refugees from the bombed-out cities traded clothes for food, or we boiled a type of German poison ivy to make spinach and searched for non-poisonous mushrooms.

In late March 1945, a huge American armored division made its way toward our village. For days, we could hear what sounded like approaching thunder. Many of the villagers prepared hiding places in the surrounding woods because German propaganda had prepared us for the worst possible American atrocities. As the U.S. Army approached, a few local Nazis marched out in front of the village with rifles to "protect" us from the Americans. Had they fired a shot, we would all have been casualties. Thank goodness, a few brave local farmers overcame this small band of Nazis and took them into custody.

Meanwhile, it was discovered that my mother was the only person in our village who spoke English, having worked for a year before the war started taking care of small children outside of London following her graduation from a teacher's college in Frankfurt. Consequently, she and the mayor stood alone at the edge of town, waiting for the tank brigade to arrive. All the villagers were requested to hang white sheets from their windows as a sign of surrender.

With Mom as translator, the mayor conferred with the American officer in charge, who selected our courtyard for his headquarters. The Russian prisoners of war were released and transported out of town by truck. Since we had treated the Russians kindly, we were not subjected to looting or any other difficulties that other parts of Germany experienced. We were actually relieved by the American capture of our little village. No more strafing by dive-bombers. No more aircraft dropping their ammunition as they returned to England or to other safe havens. And, also, soldiers offered Steve and me chocolate and chewing gum.

Although our daily anguish and danger had subsided, other areas of Germany were not as fortunate. Entire cities were sometimes demolished in a single night. Hostilities continued until May 1945, when the Germans surrendered.

Matthias Alexander, journalist for the *Frankfurter Allgemeine*, recently reported on the devastating Allied raids on my hometown of Frankfurt, Germany during the time of March 1944 to March

1945. On the evening of March 18, 1944, in a matter of one hour and fifteen minutes, 750 allied planes had dropped approximately 663,000 bombs on the city. The remains of some of the four hundred plus dead buried under the wreckage were not found until well after the war ended. The remainder of the old, historic part of the city was destroyed on the evening of March 22, 1944, causing a firestorm, exacting a toll of 1000 plus deaths. By March of 1945, half of the remaining 270,000 inhabitants were without homes.

Toward the end of the summer of 1945, my mother could finally begin the long processing and preparation for our eventual immigration to the United States. We made numerous trips through bombed-out ruins to the United States Consulate in Frankfurt, where we endured thorough health screenings, including x-rays. Other than being severely undernourished, my brother and I were in fairly good physical shape, aided by the fact that we had spent the last years of the war in a rural atmosphere where, occasionally, generous farm neighbors shared with us an occasional egg or loaf of bread. However, I had to have my tonsils removed and was treated for a severe case of dermatitis.

The consulate staff also queried and briefed us on our future life in the States while making background checks. Fortunately, I had missed being inducted into the Hitler Youth Group by a few months, for that would have delayed our departure considerably.

By early summer of 1946, we were almost ready to begin the lengthy journey to the United States. After spending almost a week in the I.G. Farben building in Frankfurt, listening to lectures on various aspects of U.S. life, my brother and I felt a little concerned about going to a country where we didn't speak English and going to school with children who might have suffered from having loved ones killed by Germans during the war. We thought it was strange that we were required to attend "denazification" sessions since we had never been Nazis. The Americans confiscated a chapter from my history book about Hitler and WWII that I wanted to take to the States as a keepsake.

Finally, saying a sad farewell to our grandmother in Frankfurt, Mom, Steve, and I boarded a train for the northern German town of Bremen. American Army trucks transported us and our few belongings from the *Bahnhof* to a military facility where we again received a thorough orientation to life in the United States, viewing films and listening to more lectures on the cultural aspects of our new home.

On August 21, we sailed from Bremerhaven aboard a converted U.S. Army troopship and headed out into the North Sea. We were overwhelmed by the delicious food. During the war, a tiny bag of sugar had to last several months, but now, we could heap unlimited spoonfuls of sugar on our hot cereal. A special treat was a cup of ice cream with dinner each evening.

Men and women slept in separate compartments. I was assigned the top bunk with eight men under me, which was fortunate because so many were seasick and regurgitated their food on those sleeping below them. Unfortunately, though, during one night of rough sea in the English Channel, I fell from my top bunk onto the floor and suffered a concussion.

I spent as much time as possible on deck, getting fresh air and playing games with the other boys, as well as reading and playing my block flute, one of the few possessions I was allowed to take with me. We passed a number of ships and freighters on the way.

Ten days into the journey, we discovered small dots on the horizon. "Those are the crests of New York skyscrapers," someone explained.

My brother and I watched with excitement as the skyline loomed larger. At the same time, we felt some anxiety as we anticipated our reunion with a father whom neither Steve nor I could remember. Mom comforted us with assurances of a better and safer life, with ample food in a place where there were no air raids or other perilous threats.

We stood on deck, awed as the ship approached endless tall skyscrapers and passed by the majestic Statue of Liberty. Carefully, a tugboat pulled the ship into Pier 88. When a "stranger" rushed up to give my mom a hug, we knew it must be our dad. A new chapter in our lives had begun.

After spending a few nights with my godmother on Long Island, we boarded a train to Cincinnati where my father had set up residence. My mother enrolled us in school almost immediately.

Much to our surprise, both students and teachers welcomed us warmly. I matriculated with students of this class through both junior high and, later, through Withrow Senior High School.

Upon graduation, I was fortunate to receive a scholarship to the University of Cincinnati, which made it possible to continue my education while living at home. I pursued a Liberal Arts education, taking enough methods courses to certify in secondary education and to graduate in 1958. When the head of the placement service announced that they could not place many of the secondary social studies majors, I was shocked. Fortunately, there was a great need for elementary teachers, and Ohio granted immediate temporary certification in this field to teachers who enrolled in a two-year program of summer and night school. Thereby, I interviewed for and was offered a position teaching fifth grade in the Deer Park Schools.

I am certain that my lack of elementary training and experience presented an initial challenge for my students and parents. However, we all made it through that first year with a substantial rise in tests scores. The credit goes to my caring principal and mentor, Howard Basinger, who never gave up on me. He and his family have become lifelong friends. I continued teaching at Deer Park for two more years, thoroughly enjoying the experience. I will never forget those great students and supportive parents.

[2]

Okinawa

One snowy January evening in 1960, while I was teaching fifth grade in Deer Park, a suburb of Cincinnati, and finishing my Master's at Miami of Ohio in Oxford, my attention focused on an article in the *Cincinnati Enquirer* entitled, "Teach Overseas and See the World." Over thirteen years had passed since I left my native Germany as a young boy, and I often wondered what it looked like today. This might be the opportunity I needed for a return visit.

Four weeks later, I arrived at the downtown Federal Building for an interview with Mr. Herman Search, superintendent of the Department of Defense Schools based in Frankfurt, Germany. He seemed very interested in my background as I shared my life in Frankfurt during World War II, describing how our house was destroyed during a British air raid in 1943, so I was pleased that at the end of our interview, he told me he would see me in Germany.

A month later, a telegram arrived at my home.

I tore it open to read, "Welcome to the Department of Defense Dependents Schools. You have been assigned to Okinawa."

Okinawa! Not Frankfurt? Where on earth was Okinawa? I had my heart set on going to Germany.

But after the initial disappointment wore off, I took my atlas down from the shelf and located a small island trailing south below Japan in an arc toward Taiwan and Hong Kong. The largest of the Ryukyuan archipelago, this spot on the map began to excite me with its possibilities of traveling while teaching in the exotic Far East. Like the many colleagues I would meet throughout the next forty-five years, I seized this opportunity for adventure.

In sharing my news with my students, we studied together the history and geography of Okinawa, learning that this 67-mile stretch of mountainous land had been the scene of one of the most violent battles of World War II. While I was hiding in the cellars of Germany, evading Allied bombing raids, the school children of Okinawa were cowering in caves, trembling in fear of the American invaders. We read about the battle of Iwo Jima nearby and the raising of the American flag there in victory.

I subsequently had to pass a physical and be inoculated numerous times for various tropical diseases. I also sold my new 1959 Fiat and began loading a few of my worldly possessions into a steamer trunk, for I was authorized to ship only 300 pounds. As the school year drew to a close, I finished my Master's degree and was inducted into Phi Delta Kappa, the Education Honorary Society. My little fifth graders sent me off with warm farewells, good wishes, and a new suitcase. Before leaving, I promised to send my mother a letter each week—a practice of describing my adventures overseas that I continued until her death in 1992.

My DoDDS career was launched on July 27 with a good high school friend, Bob Davis, driving my mother and me to Cincinnati's Union Station. There I joined up with two other teachers assigned to Okinawa for the train trip to Chicago and San Francisco. At Fort Mason Army Base, in California, we new employees were kept waiting many hours in line to fill out numerous forms and sign assorted paperwork, processing us into the Department of Defense Dependents Schools system. When all was completed, they informed me I would be teaching a fifth-grade class at Machinato, a location approximately eight miles from the Okinawan capital city of Naha.

So much had happened in so short a time since I spotted that obscure article in the newspaper, offering the chance "to see the World." I stood at the ship's railing, wind in my face, as the *General Gaffey* set sail under the Golden Gate Bridge into the spacious waters of the Pacific, precisely at 1400 hours—I remembered to convert two p.m. civilian time to military time—on August 2, 1960.

For the next eighteen days, approximately 150 teachers and 300 military family members would share one of the most modern ships the Army utilized to send dependents overseas. I roomed with three other male teachers in a cabin on the third deck above the waterline. Several days out, the waters became a little choppy, and a few of my compatriots suffered seasickness, but I was fortunate to escape. The food was excellent and buffets were available throughout the day, or we could choose three regular meals. Except for scheduled faculty meetings, we might have been on a cruise, enjoying moonlight dances on the deck, viewing movies, attending chapel. The crew even held an initiation for those of us who had never crossed the International Date Line. In all, we had ample time to read or simply chat with the other passengers and get acquainted.

A day and a half stopover in Yokohama Harbor, Japan, provided a welcome relief from the lengthy journey. Hattie Higa, a good friend who spoke fluent Japanese, took a few of us teachers by subway to Tokyo where we stayed overnight, shopped at the Ginza, and walked to the Emperor's palace.

The General Gaffey finally docked at Naha, Okinawa on August 17 at eleven in the morning. No one was authorized to leave the ship until their turn was called. We teachers waited as the loudspeaker announced the priorities for disembarkation:

officers and their families, enlisted men and their families, single soldiers, pets, and finally, schoolteachers. We hoped this would be no indication of our future status in the military community. Actually, we would be well accepted by the military families, and I would enjoy many evening meals with the parents of my fifth graders.

Doug McRae, the principal from Machinato, greeted us new teachers and took us by bus to the BOQs—a military acronym for Bachelor Officers' Quarters. Most of the female teachers lived in a large forty- person structure just down the hill from us males. The BOQ I shared with three other men was a little cement structure with four bedrooms, a bathroom on either side of the building, and a living room of adequate size. My room faced west with a magnificent view of the East China Sea. BOQ life would prove especially conducive to building lifelong friendships, as almost every evening, the teachers took turns gathering in each other's rooms to chat. In Okinawan fashion, we sat on pillow cushions placed on the floor and shared episodes from our past lives, especially interesting since we all came from different areas of the United States.

Settling in for the night at the BOQ, though, could turn into somewhat of a challenge. In order to enjoy a good sleep, I had to exterminate what seemed like hundreds of little crawlers as well as some good- sized spiders and roaches.

The morning following my arrival in Okinawa, I remember looking out my BOQ window to see our ship, the Gaffey, disappearing beneath the horizon, sailing back, I realized with a twinge of homesickness, toward the United States. But unique adventures awaited us new arrivals. That afternoon, the island was struck by the fierce winds and driving rain of an approaching typhoon. I recall walking from the little snack bar to the BOQ, placing one foot forward and being pushed two feet backwards by the strong gales. Fortunately, the full force of that typhoon turned away from Okinawa.

With a few free days before the start of school, everyone from the *Gaffey* was eager to explore the capital, Naha, which was only minutes away by bus. Since I was one of only three male teachers on the faculty, I never left the area without the companionship of at least four to ten female teachers who thought I might offer a little protection while they browsed in all the little shops.

Early on, we new teachers were introduced to social life in Okinawa. We dined at the fabulous Officers' Clubs in the area—the "Top of the Rock Club" at Fort Buckner, the "Wing" and the "Naha Fighters' Clubs" among others, which presented musical entertainment from the U.S. and served excellent food for very reasonable prices, made possible through profits from slot machines. To experience the local food outside our little compound, we sometimes gathered at a restaurant made famous by the movie Teahouse of the August Moon, which featured traditional Japanese fare, music, and entertainment. On weekends, our social lives consisted of going on tours, shopping in Naha, and partying.

Our first duty, though, was to provide American dependents with a quality American education. Machinato School consisted of two long military barracks near the East China Sea. A typical day began with a 7:00 breakfast at the little cafeteria near our quarters that we teachers aptly named "The Greasy Spoon." I usually feasted on powdered scrambled eggs and potatoes.

From there, teachers either walked or took a bus to school. The approximately eight hundred students arrived by bus at 8:45. Recess was 10:15 to 10:30 and teachers ate lunch with the students in shifts at noon. School was dismissed at 3 pm. I was fortunate to have a great class of eager learners and rarely experienced a discipline problem.

I remember that during the first week of school, I attended an island-wide meeting of the Parent-Teacher Association at which free cocktails were served. This was a novel experience for me, since in Cincinnati, teachers were once chastised for having a beer during meetings of our faculty bowling league.

In addition to my teaching duties, I was tasked with supervising the safety patrol, serving as head P.E. teacher, coaching the track team, as well as performing "other duties as assigned," a catchphrase, I learned, that in DoDDS covers most anything the principal might want done. The culminating event of the sports season, an island-wide Junior Olympics in the spring, became my responsibility to coach and organize. The principal informed me, "I expect you to field a winning team." Fortunately, I was allowed to enlist GIs to assist with the coaching duties.

On weekends, we teachers enjoyed exploring the island and its villages. For one of my first Saturday excursions, a group of friends and I rode by bus to the southern tip of Okinawa. Our prime destination was "Suicide Cliff," site of the last stronghold by the Japanese in World War II. The Battle of Okinawa had raged for eighty days following the American invasion on April 1, 1945. In desperation, the Japanese Commanding General, seeing that the battle was lost, ordered his troops to "Fight to the last, and die for the Eternal Cause!" Then, following traditional samurai ritual, as the moon was setting in the dark hours of the morning on June 23, he and his staff officer committed *hari-kari* on the cliff overlooking the sea. We sightseers spent some time enjoying the view and looking at the monument that sits atop the graves of the fallen generals.

At Itoman, a fishing village twelve miles south of Naha, we were told that since the men were gone on fishing excursions for weeks at a time, the Okinawan women were totally in charge of day-to- day government functions. When the men returned, the women purchased their catch and sold the fish in the market, keeping the profits for themselves.

Once a year the villagers of Yonabaru, located on the Pacific side of the island, engage in a gigantic tug-of-war. Dressed in their traditional costumes, the villagers attempt to interlock two ropes made of rice straw representing the male and the female. The ropes are about three feet in diameter and as long as one and a half American football fields, ending in giant loops. When they are attached to each other, the men and women start pulling. The original contest, the guidebooks say, began centuries ago to scare insects out of the rice fields, and tradition claims that when the women win, the next year's harvest will be good.

Another spot popular with both teachers and the military was the American-operated Okuma Recreation Center, near the northern end of the island. Getting onto a crowded local bus while a sturdy Okinawan woman, acting as a pusher, shoved us right into the middle of the passengers was quite an adventure, but the tranquil ocean beach setting against a backdrop of low mountain ranges made it worthwhile.

I always had the pleasure of having several female companions on these excursions. However, I soon learned that I wouldn't have all the women to myself, for officers often invited them to attend military functions. Some, though, returned to going to movies or the club with this skinny young school teacher when they realized they had dated a married soldier.

School holidays allowed for more extensive travel. During Thanksgiving break, thirty of us teachers descended on Taipei, Taiwan. We toured several Buddhist temples and rode a bus through the countryside to Taichung, viewing farmers harvesting their rice crops, aided by water buffalo. A special treat was our visit to a local school founded by Madame Chiang Kai-shek where we heard the children sing about returning to the Mainland and throwing out the communists.

After our return, I wasn't feeling well. The doctor told me I was infected with some kind of bug which would have to work itself out through the many feet of my intestines. I remember forcing down chocolate ice cream for breakfast, lunch, and dinner, and that I lost a lot of weight. The process of healing took most of December; however, I never missed a day of school.

At the start of our winter break, December 21, friends and I departed Okinawa on CAT, the Nationalist China Airlines, arriving in Hong Kong at noon. We had a brief time to spend in the capital city, Victoria, and to take the Star Ferry to Kowloon. From there, we toured the New Territories with a stop at the Communist Chinese border.

Two days later, we flew on Air India, with stops in Rangoon, Burma and Calcutta, to New Delhi. We explored old Moslem palaces, the largest mosque in India, and the Red Fort, built by the Moguls. Our next stop was Agra, home of the magnificent Taj Mahal, to marvel at its white marble inlaid with semiprecious stones. Banaras-on-the-Ganges, India's holy city, was our final Indian destination. We watched as thousands of pilgrims bathed in the river, while downstream, hundreds of bodies wrapped in sheets were being cremated.

Because of my family's friendship with a chiropractor in Cincinnati who had treated Mahatma Gandhi in years past, I experienced a special treat most tourists never have. This doctor arranged for me to visit a family residence of a physician in Delhi.

En route home to Okinawa, we visited the King's Place in Bangkok and enjoyed a trip on the canal to the Floating Market. While spending New Year's Day in Hong Kong, we feasted on a scrumptious multi-course meal at the famous Floating Restaurant.

In January 1961, the political situation in Laos and VietNam became more serious, and our troops on Okinawa, which included the parents of my students, were placed on full alert. They waited, ready to move out on half an hour's notice. Ships were fully loaded with military equipment while jets continually circled overhead.

Meanwhile, many of us were excited about the upcoming inauguration of John Fitzgerald Kennedy on January 20. My students and I prepared a bulletin board which featured the youthful and charismatic new president and his talented, newly installed cabinet.

By the end of January, the coaches I had recruited from the military and I started getting serious about the upcoming track meet which would include forty-, fifty-, and sixty-yard dashes, high jump, broad jump, softball throw, and relays. We separated the students into classes by height, weight, and age and began their training.

News of transfers within the DoDDS system started arriving about this time, and the two-year teachers received offers for the following school year to France, the Philippines, Germany, Morocco, Libya, Pakistan, and Japan. However, I was on a one-year leave of absence from Deer Park and had decided to return home in the summer to continue with my graduate courses.

During our spring break, a large group of us teachers made a trip together to Japan. Although it was quite strenuous going from place to place in a short period of time, we enjoyed ourselves, staying overnight in small Japanese inns and sleeping on the floor on futons. My friends and I were the only three men on the trip, other than the three tour guides, traveling with fifty-six women. Gentlemen that we were, the six of us were expected to unload seventy plus suitcases through the train windows and doors at each location. Since the trains stopped only two-and-a-half minutes in each station, we often barely finished before the train pulled out. However, the tour guides rewarded us on our last day of the trip with a full-course dinner and dancing in a plush Tokyo nightclub accompanied by beautiful hostesses.

The rainy season on Okinawa arrived in early May, bringing with it the fringe of one typhoon with winds clocked at ninety miles an hour that, fortunately, turned toward Hong Kong. In the days leading up to the Junior Olympics, our athletes missed only two practices due to weather.

Finally, the big day of the island-wide track meet arrived. The events began at ten a.m. By two o'clock, Machinato Elementary lagged behind, in third place. Kadena Elementary had a larger student population than we did. However, our cheering section was the loudest, and we knew we had the best athletes. With a fresh burst of determination, the Machinato team gave it their all, winning almost every event during the remaining hour of the meet.

Headlines in the local newspaper shouted, "MACHINATO SCHOOL GRABS TOP HONORS IN JUNIOR OLYMPICS!" Weeks of hard work had paid off. The students were elated about the outcome. Mr. Harry Frey, the Okinawa superintendent, presented the team with a trophy, honoring both the team and coaches with a victory celebration the following week.

As always, the last month of school was busy with culminating activities. I sponsored an end-of-the-year banquet for the safety patrols to present them with their certificates. My principal presented three other teachers and me with Ryukyu Army Outstanding Service Certificates. I believe my award was more for performing the extra duty assignments; however, my class had achieved excellent scores on the national achievement tests.

June 5, all of us teachers were sent to the Civilian Personnel Office to "out process." On the last day of school, June 6, each homeroom celebrated with a party. Since I was one of the few teachers who had opted to take a ship back to the States, most of the students told me they would come down to the dock in Naha at the end of June to see me off.

On June 7, two planes left from Kadena, transporting the majority of teachers on their thirty-hour trek to Travis Air Force Base near San Francisco, going home for the summer. I was told that they would not allow me to see the teachers off because we were still officially on duty. However, at the last minute, the assistant principal felt sorry for me and drove me to Kadena Air Base to watch my friends depart.

Months before, I had met a tall, good-looking teacher on shipboard who would be on my staff. She had told me then, "I am going to work in Okinawa for one year only. I am engaged to be married, and we have set the wedding date for next August. I want you to be my friend during this year. However, don't get too serious. I will definitely marry my fiancé." True to her word, we had become good friends, and now she was going home to be married. I saw that she had partially ascended the steps of the plane when I belatedly arrived at the airport. After I called out her name, she hurried back down, and we hugged on the tarmac to the cheers of the many bystanders. Two weeks after I had returned to Cincinnati, I received her wedding invitation.

My final three weeks on Okinawa were a little lonely, but there were enough folks left to enjoy the touring and club life. At the end of June, I wrote home,

"This is my last letter from 'The Rock.' I am looking forward to coming home; however, I am really sad to leave. The place grows on you. The weather has been great; sunshine every day and there is a slight breeze blowing. Last night some of the teachers hosted a sayonara dinner for me. Monday is a bachelor sayonara in Naha. The Okinawa culture teacher at our school invited me and a few of the teachers for dinner. I remember meeting her during Orientation Week at the beginning of school. We both reached the front door of the school at the same time and I held it open for her. She insisted that I go through first because this was the local custom. Unfortunately, I will soon have to observe American customs again."

My students and their parents gave me an overwhelming send-off when my ship departed from the port in Naha. According to custom, I stood on the deck and tossed colored streamers down to the folks who bid me farewell. I will never forget those ribbons breaking one by one as parents and kids waved goodbye and my ship sailed out to sea. A Navy nurse on board shared with me that she had seen many local farewells, but this was one of the most impressive.

[3]

Kaiserslautern, Germany

The year following my return from Okinawa, I taught again at Deer Park and resided in Cincinnati with my parents, honoring my one-year leave of absence. Although I had a great teaching assignment, I realized early on that my heart was overseas. In January, 1962, I interviewed again with DoDDS, and this time the acceptance telegram assigned me to Germany.

On August 8, 1962, I sailed from New York Harbor on the *General Patch*. The weather was cloudy and somewhat stormy throughout the trip as the ship sailed the northern route past Newfoundland, along the coast of Scotland, and down the North Sea into Bremerhaven. By request, I taught a German language class to any military families or DoDDS personnel on board who wanted to attend, so the time passed quickly. Some were so eager to learn German phrases that they bothered me with questions all day long, and I had to develop a few avoidance techniques.

Upon our arrival, August 26, we new teachers received our specific orders. They assigned me to Kaiserslautern, a city in southwestern Germany, not too distant from the French border. All of us from the *General Patch* started south on the same American troop train, but in Frankfurt, some railroad cars were diverted east; others, west and south toward our ultimate destinations.

Those of us disembarking at the Kaiserslautern train station were met by two teachers and a bus driver who escorted us to the Bachelor Officers' Quarters (BOQs) on the Vogelweh Army compound. They took me to a forty-man converted barracks where I inherited a freshly painted room with a new desk, lamp, big cupboard, and two chairs. The bathroom I would share with a veteran teacher.

After unloading our suitcases, we were escorted to the Officers' Club, which turned out to be an excellent dining facility with a bar and accommodation for parties and conferences. Teachers, urged to join the Club for monthly dues of $5.00, soon discovered it to be the center of our social lives and an excellent place to meet the parents and military commanders. I was duly impressed that on one of my first nights in Kaiserslautern, I sat just two tables down from General Freeman, Commander of Army Europe.

Kaiserslautern Elementary #1
1962-63

The city of Kaiserslautern hosted one of the largest American military communities in Europe at the time, and Kaiserslautern #1, the elementary school where I would be teaching, had over 1600 students enrolled. Principal Jane Ritter, a retired Army major, ran a tight ship. My fourth-grade class contained twenty-five students. We classroom teachers were responsible for our own art and music; however, specialists in these areas served five schools by scheduling after-class workshops and occasional lessons. Students received afternoon instruction in German culture and conversation from a local teacher.

The exchange rate was 4.20 *Deutschmarks* (DM) to the dollar, so although our salaries were modest, we could take advantage of the excellent rate to travel on the weekends and to experience the local culture. One of my first evenings in Kaiserslautern, a group of us teachers went downtown to the *Pfalzkeller*, a restaurant serving delicious, traditional local fare. It was great fun to live in a country where I had mastered the language even if, in the beginning, I had to pay close attention due to the local dialect.

One of my first challenges was taking the German driver's test, made up of seventy-five questions and fifty road signs, which I passed, missing only four. However, I decided not to purchase a car during the first year because nearly every town and village in the country was connected by bus or train.

Over the Labor Day weekend, a colleague I had met on the ship joined me in making a pilgrimage to my hometown of Frankfurt. Despite all the years since I had last seen it, the train station where my mother, brother, and I had departed for Bremen and our voyage to the United States in 1946 looked the same, except that parts of the roof had been repaired. My friend and I rode streetcar #16 to the *Hauptwache* where we walked across the plaza to the cathedral in which a number of Holy Roman Emperors had been crowned during the Middle Ages. Miraculously, the cathedral had been spared the bombings of the war.

Next, we crossed the Main River to Sachsenhausen, the suburb where my family had lived during the war, and climbed the long winding route to the top of the *Muehlberg* where my old home had been at *Miltenbergerstrasse* 3. I was relieved to see it had been restored pretty much to its original dimensions. In the years to come, I was often drawn by a sense of nostalgia to climb that long hill again and revisit my roots.

On Sunday we attended services at the *Dreikoenigskirche*, located on the Main River opposite the cathedral—the church where I was christened. As one of Germany's oldest churches, it was originally Roman Catholic, then converted after the

Reformation. I recounted to my friend the story of one memorable service in 1942 when the pastor was removed from the pulpit by two Nazis for making anti-Hitler references in his sermon.

The following weekend, I traveled to Steinbach in Westerwald, the little village where my family resided from the time bombs destroyed our apartment until the war ended. I was delighted that our former neighbors remembered me and invited me to a hearty meal of cold cuts, potato salad, delicious dark bread, and a field salad. I discovered that my good childhood friend, Norbert Heep, and his wife operated a truck farm, rising at 4 am each morning of the week, except Sundays, to deliver vegetables to markets in Frankfurt. He and I attended the little village church together on Sunday, then ate lunch in a local *Gasthaus* before he drove me to Limburg where I boarded a train back to Kaiserslautern.

My other fall weekend excursions included the historic old city of Heidelberg and the Oktoberfest in Munich, where the festival grounds were lined with huge tents representing various German beer companies. Hundreds of folks crowded into each, singing along with Bavarian bands and consuming huge steins full of beer. On nearly every trip, I ran into teacher friends I knew from Okinawa who had transferred to various locations throughout Germany.

One of my best decisions and an important part of my German social life during this first year was to join the Kaiserslautern *Musikverein*, or music club, an old, established organization that had been in existence for over a hundred years. Following every Wednesday evening's rehearsal in preparation for two annual concerts, members assembled in a local restaurant for an evening snack and wine. We also went on various excursions and performed concerts in village squares as far away as Nancy, France.

My bass singing partner at the music club was Jakob Becker, and we soon became great friends. His parents and sister, Ursula, literally adopted Liz Morris, who was also a club member, and me into their family, and we have visited them throughout the years. Ursula later married Peter Haas and, with their vivacious daughter, Andrea still keep up the tradition of telephoning us on our birthdays and hosting us whenever we are in Germany.

Most DoDDS teachers are eager to avail themselves of traveling opportunities at each new assignment, and I was no different. I spent my four- day Thanksgiving break on a whirlwind trip to Italy with a good friend, John Bennett, the high school music teacher. Wednesday after class, we hurried to Heidelberg where we boarded a sleeper car on the Copenhagen-Milano Express, arriving in Milano Thursday morning. We continued on to Florence before disembarking to tour the cathedral, the old bridge with the goldsmith's workshop, and an art gallery. Then we took another train to Rome, and although it was late in the evening, we found a pleasant room at the YMCA for $5.00.

Friday morning John and I traveled further south to the ancient site of Pompeii and wandered amid the excavated ruins once buried under the volcanic ash of Mount Vesuvius, looming on the horizon. We stopped briefly in Naples to board a bus headed downtown for a view of the bay before returning to Rome. With the rest of our vacation time, we visited the Roman Coliseum, St. Peter's Cathedral, and the Vatican. Two tired teachers boarded the train for Germany on Sunday evening.

On the ride back, we met and talked with Peter Sellers, the English actor who starred in the movie *The Mouse That Roared*, before crawling into our couchette bunks to get some sleep. Too soon, the rising sun reflecting on the magnificent Swiss Alps awakened us. We arrived in Kaiserslautern at 5 am, just in time to start school. John and I definitely decided not to attempt seeing an entire country in one weekend again. However, at the time, neither of us was aware how long we would remain in Europe.

In early December, I traveled to Cologne to visit Uncle Voss, my mother's brother, and his wife and two children. My cousin Ursula was a high school teacher who had written a number of articles on art and culture for various major German newspapers. Her brother, Werner, was a medical doctor in nearby Aachen. Between long walks, we visited the immense Gothic cathedral in Cologne, an art museum, and Konrad Adenauer's residence, the German "White House," in Bonn.

During winter break, I joined sixty-five participants, mostly DoDDS teachers, on a trip through Spain, Portugal, and Morocco. We first flew from Frankfurt to Madrid. Then, we traveled by bus to Toledo, a historic city whose sand-colored houses and medieval cathedral tower above the Tagus River, and visited the home of the artist El Greco, located in the heart of the Jewish Quarter and now converted into a museum. We celebrated Christmas Day with a delicious dinner in the quaint mountain village of Guarda, Portugal before continuing on to Lisbon. Our tour included a boat crossing of the Strait of Gibraltar to Tangiers, Morocco. A guide showed us the city on foot and let us shop in the little quaint shops of the crowded bazaar. Before leaving this old Muslim country, we made a 150-mile day trip by taxi into the interior to see a little mountain village almost untouched by modern civilization.

Our holiday trip concluded with a drive to Barcelona, on through southern France to Geneva, Switzerland. We paused there long enough for a sightseeing tour of the United Nations palace before continuing along Lake Geneva to Basel. Eventually we reached Karlsruhe in Germany, where we boarded a train which took us to Kaiserslautern.

During the cold and snowy winter months that year, I kept occupied with choir practices, parties, local weekend excursions, serious teaching, and preparations for a school Science Fair and Open House. The highlights of the German winter social calendar are New Year's and *Fasching* balls, a time for music, dancing, and elegant costumes, leading up to the start of Lent.

Prior to this time, I had talked occasionally with the young sixth grade teacher from Moultrie, Georgia who worked upstairs, above my fourth-grade classroom. She was good-looking, and vivacious, and when we met at music club rehearsals and other social events, I liked her southern accent. Our relationship deepened after we attended a Fasching ball with our music club and danced part of the night away. Liz and I became engaged during the last week in March.

Spring break arrived, and Liz and I joined a sizable group leaving Kaiserslautern on six busses for a ten-day tour to Russia. We immediately noticed the poverty of the countryside after crossing the German- Czech border. However, in Prague, the people seemed freer and better dressed than anywhere else behind the Iron Curtain. We rode on to Warsaw, Poland and had a day of sightseeing, including the old Jewish Quarters.

Our busses were thoroughly searched when we crossed the USSR border in the town of Brest, and we were joined by two knowledgeable and attractive Intourist guides who would accompany us throughout our tour. Both were teachers and spoke excellent English. We felt they answered our many questions very diplomatically.

The bus continued on to Minsk and Smolensk, where we visited an Orthodox Church, before arriving in Moscow. For me, the highlights in Moscow included seeing the Kremlin and Lenin's Tomb on Red Square, shopping in the GUM Department

Store, and attending an evening performance of *Spartacus* at the Bolshoi Theater.

The following morning, our group of teachers visited a Russian school. The teacher of the foreign language class I visited told us that the students had studied English for only four months. Nevertheless, two girls gave ten-minute talks about themselves and their families in English.

Afterwards, our tour group boarded a plane for Leningrad to visit Peter's Palace and the Hermitage Museum. Another flight returned us to Prague, where Liz shopped for and bought a set of crystal before boarding the bus for the lengthy journey back to Kaiserslautern. We both agreed that we would not board another bus for a long time.

As the school year drew to a close, Liz and I began preparation for our marriage. We were required to fill out numerous forms for both the United States and the German governments, including getting permission from our school principal and the Army chaplain. In addition, we had to pay 10% net of one month's salary to the German government for the required civil ceremony.

On June 7, 1963, one hundred fifty guests, mostly teachers, attended our wedding at the Vogelweh Chapel. Lee Bartley, assistant principal- just-promoted-to-principal that spring, gave Liz away. One of my fourth graders served as the flower girl, and a student in Liz's class was the ring bearer. A cousin, Jerry Voss, and his wife, Helga, represented the family.

Liz and I had booked a German tour to Scandinavia, which departed the weekend after school ended. We rode a sleeper car to Hamburg, flew on to Bardufoss, and rode a bus along the coastline to Tromso, Norway. From there we traveled by ship through the northern fiords to Hammerfest on the Arctic Circle, the most northern city in the world, where we enjoyed the magnificent scenery in the "Land of the Midnight Sun."

From Hammerfest, the bus took us through Finland and south to Stockholm, Sweden. After a couple of days of sightseeing, the tour continued by train to Copenhagen for visits to Tivoli Gardens and up the coast to Hamlet's castle.

As a married couple, the Army now provided Liz and I with a spacious apartment on the Vogelweh post. It was fully furnished, including such items as silverware and champagne and wine glasses. We also purchased a little white Volkswagen bug and enjoyed making quick trips throughout the scenic German countryside.

That summer, after getting settled in our military quarters, we decided to make a quick trip to the British Isles. We drove through Luxembourg and Brussels, Belgium to Calais, France, where we boarded a ferry for the two-hour ride to Dover. I found it challenging to drive on the left side of the road in England, but we managed successfully. We spent three days in London seeing the major landmarks and attending a couple of plays. Driving on to Scotland, we marveled at steep, green slopes, spotted with sheep, which seemed to touch the sky. From Edinburgh, we made several local excursions through the highlands to Loch Lomond, including Robert Burns' country.

Before the school year 1963-1964 began, I received word that I had been accepted for a counseling position at Kaiserslautern High School.

Kaiserslautern High School
1963-64

In the fall of 1963, the counseling staff at Kaiserslautern High had to register and schedule over 1600 students within a two-week period. Responsible for eighth and ninth grade counseling and scheduling, I managed the process after a few false starts and bumps. Once classes began, I spent most of each day holding individual and family counseling sessions and registering and escorting new arrivals to their classrooms.

In addition to my counseling duties, I was given the challenging assignment of teaching two sections of remedial English. These students, required to take both their regular English class and my remedial class, were not at all happy about the prospect. On Monday, Wednesday, and Friday, I taught fifteen girls, and on Tuesday and Thursday, I taught twenty-five boys, opposite their PE classes. There were no textbooks, so I made up my own materials. The girls were cooperative and made a gallant effort to improve. The boys, however, were another story. I occasionally threatened them with staying after school, which meant they would have to take a late bus home, a hardship for those living in outlying areas.

Liz and I found that our social life consisted of many teacher parties and invitations to dinner. There always seemed to be a group ready to travel on weekends or to enjoy eating out at a local restaurant. A bowling league was organized after school, and once we went with several friends to Bad Dürkheim, the largest wine and sausage festival in Europe. I also attended most of the athletic events, which improved my relations with students.

One day, Liz informed me that she was expecting sometime in April and arranged to take a couple of weeks off from work prior to the birth of our daughter plus six weeks of recuperation afterwards. Kathryn Renate Ellinger was born on April 28, 1964, at the huge Landstuhl American Military Hospital near Kaiserslautern. We waited impatiently until Kathryn was six weeks old and eligible to travel on a MAC flight so we could go home for the summer to show off our precious baby girl.

After landing at McGuire Air Force Base, we rode a bus into Philadelphia and finally arrived in Cincinnati on June 20th, where we visited with my parents for a couple of weeks before going on to Liz's parents' home in Georgia. I enjoyed spending time with my new in-laws. Liz's dear mother, Vista Morris, welcomed me with open arms. Her dad was a tobacco and cotton farmer in the town of Moultrie. As I joined him at tobacco auctions and attempted to assist him with his daily chores, he never became impatient teaching this city boy the ropes.

While we were in the States, I completed my summer counseling practicum course at Miami University in Oxford, Ohio. Before our vacation ended, I received a telegram from our superintendent offering me a Teacher/Principal position in Weierhof, Germany.

Weierhof American School
1964-65

Home again at our apartment on the post at Vogelweh, I discovered that my daily commute from Kaiserslautern to Weierhof was approximately forty- five minutes on the winding two-lane highway. Surrounded by rich farmland and rolling hills with a view of the *Donnersberg*, the highest peak in the Palatinate, the village of Weierhof consisted of several large farmhouses and barns in addition to a Mennonite *Gymnasium*, our classical secondary school, with dormitories for students who commuted from the surrounding area. Ten four-story buildings made up the housing area for the American families and military members whose children would attend Weierhof American School with its staff of four.

The school building, set in the middle of the military housing area, contained a principal's office, three classrooms, a supply room, and a library. The faculty consisted of two excellent teachers, Rosemary Friley and Hildegard Hofacker, plus an efficient secretary, Frau Schumann. My duties as principal were to administer the school as well as teach a combination fifth/ sixth grade class. We all worked together to register students, put up bulletin boards, and distribute new textbooks in time for opening day.

Interruptions to my teaching schedule commonly occurred while I took phone calls from the district office or talked to parents wandering into the building without appointments. The paratroopers who used the area surrounding the school for a landing site caused another distraction. Often in the middle of the afternoon, the sky darkened as they practiced their jumps, and we teachers had difficulty getting the children back on task.

At the end of September, I was invited to the large European Administrators' Conference at the Rest and Recreation Center for American servicemen and their families in Berchtesgaden, a beautiful Alpine town in southern Bavaria. It was a splendid opportunity to meet the principals of the European Region which extended from Iceland in the north to Ethiopia in the south. We heard excellent speakers from the United States on all aspects of curriculum and administration and participated in workshops designed to assist newcomers like me prepare for day-to-day administrative tasks.

In mid-October, the three of us faculty members held successful parent conferences. Actually, the parents already had a good idea what transpired at school because they could see into the classrooms from their living rooms. The initial visit by the superintendent, Walter Ingram, also went well.

Christmas Trip to the Middle East

In December, some of Liz's girlfriends came from the States to visit, so I decided to join a tour trip to the Middle East. Due to bad weather, our flight was delayed in Munich, leaving us only one day in Athens to see the Acropolis and Parthenon. But from then on, the weather was perfect and the strange and unfamiliar sights were exciting.

Egypt, which reminded me a lot of India although the people were better off, was the highlight for me. Despite all I had read about them, the Egyptians were extremely friendly. Frequently, even if we bought only a few postcards, they invited us tourists into their shops for tea.

Leaving Cairo, the tour traveled to Memphis, the country's first capital, then on to Sakkara, the location of approximately fifteen pyramids with tombs of kings who had lived around 3000 BC.

Later we returned to the outskirts of Cairo, to a restaurant near the pyramids where camels were available for us to ride up a hill to the Sphinx. Unlike riding a horse, the rider sits rather precariously high atop the camel's hump and its spindly legs. I expected to lope along at the back of the caravan since my camel started second to last in a string of forty. But no! He just shoved all the other camels out of his way, trotting off like a horse, and I almost fell off. We completed the ride in second place.

Some of the more energetic in the group climbed all the way up the pyramids. That evening, we were treated to a sound and light performance as various pyramids were illuminated while we listened to a narrative of the different periods of history they had witnessed.

The following day's tour took us to the Egyptian Museum, where we viewed the mummy of King Tut and artifacts that had been buried with the pharaohs. The afternoon was free for us to wander through the city's main marketplace and visit one of its famous mosques.

Next, we flew down to Aswan near the Sudan border where the Russians were engaged in building the huge dam which would be completed in 1970. From the plane, our only view was of the mighty Nile River, a strip of green on either side, and nothing beyond but desert as far as the eye could see. The temperature at the Aswan Airport at 4 pm was 87 degrees, pleasantly warm compared to the winter weather we had left in Germany.

Some of our group visited a modern girls' high school in Aswan. The principal was very articulate and spoke fluent English, explaining that the school was democratically run and that students took part in the curriculum planning. Photos of Egyptian President Nasser and the Russian dictator Nikita Khrushchev were visible throughout the school because the latter had visited the year prior. Before departing, we rode a sailboat on the Nile to one of the islands consisting of a combination of botanical gardens and zoo.

We flew back up the Nile, landing at Luxor, then crossing over the river to the Valley of the Kings. This dry and desolate region contains many royal Egyptian tombs which we could explore while our guides explained the hieroglyphics found on the wall. I especially remember the tomb of Ramses VI, which was cut inside a mountain where we watched as archeologists and foremen supervised workers assembling temples from rocks laid out according to intricate blueprints.

As our tour to Egypt concluded, and Christmas Day approached, we flew to the city of Jerusalem. On the first night there, we visited an orphanage where the children performed Jordanian dances and enacted the Biblical story of the journey of Joseph and Mary by donkey to Bethlehem. The next day, we ourselves rode a bus to

Bethlehem and visited the Church of the Nativity located above the traditional site of the birth of Jesus. We also followed the traditional route that Jesus took through Jerusalem on His way to the cross, commencing with a visit to the Garden of Gethsemane on the Mount of Olives, then walking into the old city to the Church of the Holy Sepulchre. Later, our tour journeyed to the banks of the Jordan River and to the Dead Sea, so filled with accumulated silt and chemicals that one could actually sit on the water and read a book.

By the time our tour reached Damascus, Syria, I was, unfortunately, suffering from a serious intestinal infection, probably the result of eating a packed lunch on the plane from Luxor. I did manage to visit the *Al Azam* Palace and the *Umayyad* Mosque, where it is said the head of John the Baptist is buried.

Between Damascus and Beirut, the tour stopped at Baalbek, the site of ancient Greek and Roman ruins, and Byblos, the latter considered the oldest still-occupied city in the world. Beirut, Lebanon, which would eventually become a war-torn and ravaged region before the end of the century, was still a beautiful city in 1964. We stayed at a very modern hotel overlooking the Mediterranean. While there, the guide took me to the American University Hospital, but the medication I was given was not effective, and my friends on the tour told me that I had actually turned a green color. Not until I had eaten a hamburger at the American base in Munich did I fully recover.

The tour concluded in Istanbul, Turkey with a visit to the Blue Mosque, the largest in the Moslem world and so named for its mosaics of blue tiles, a look at the Bosporus Straits connecting the Mediterranean with the Black Sea, thereby dividing Europe from Asia, and stop at the magnificent Hagia Sophia Mosque, originally Christendom's greatest church for more than a millennium.

I finally regained my health after returning to Germany and to work. The school year at Weierhof proceeded without incident. In the spring, Rosemary Friley, the kindergarten/primary teacher, married Walter Lichti, a local high school teacher. They would build a beautiful home overlooking the town which Liz and I often visited in the ensuing years. The other teacher on staff, Hilde Hofacker, received a transfer to Berlin.

Liz and I were fortunate to have found an excellent babysitter for little Kathryn. *Tante* Lydia, a loyal German lady from the neighboring town of Hohenecken, became a part of our family, walking Kathryn to German kindergarten when she was small and caring for Kathryn for the first twelve years of her life. Even after we transferred to Frankfurt, *Tante* Lydia would come up by train to help us out.

Liz and I were able to get away for an enjoyable long weekend during spring break in Paris, leaving Kathryn with Lydia. After an all-night bus ride from Kaiserslautern, we visited the Louvre and toured the major sights, including the Eiffel Tower, Notre Dame Cathedral, and Napoleon's Tomb. That evening, we had front row seats for the show at the *Moulin Rouge*. The following day, we traveled out to Versailles to view its magnificent palace and gardens, returning in time for the evening show at the *Folies Bergere*.

After the school year ended in June, we spent two relaxing weeks in Rimini on the Italian Adriatic Coast. Later in the summer, I received a call from the superintendent promoting me to a full-time administrative position as Assistant Principal of Kaiserslautern Elementary School #2.

Kaiserslautern Elementary #2
1965-1968

As the 1965-66 school year got underway, Superintendent Walter Ingram asked me to continue my duties as principal of the Weierhof School in addition to my new position of assistant principal in the large Kaiserslautern Elementary School #2. Consequently, a staff car drove me to Weierhof every Thursday afternoon to accomplish the administrative tasks there.

Meanwhile, Principal Charles Jenkins assigned me the supervision of the primary grades and the special education classes at Kaiserslautern #2. (Elementary #1 was in a separate campus on the hill.) Soon new teachers arrived, some transferees from other parts of the world and many new-hires from the United States. I enjoyed meeting all the folks, assisting them in getting settled, and orienting them to our curriculum.

The entire Kaiserslautern student population numbered 4000 in a complex that included the junior high, high school, and Elementary Schools #1 and #2. Since most of Kaiserslautern Elementary #2's enrollment of 1100 students commuted from "the economy" or local towns, they arrived on one of the fifty busses that served the complex, and they stayed in the building to eat lunch in the cafeteria. The opening week of school was especially challenging as teachers and I worked to ensure that kindergarteners and first graders boarded the correct bus.

At Kaiserslautern Elementary #1, Liz, as Department Chair of six sixth grade classes, had responsibility for making out schedules and ordering supplies. Still, we were able to make a few weekend excursions in the early fall, including one to Switzerland. We also drove to the Black Forest where we ordered wooden kitchen furniture, carved with characters from Grimm Brothers' Fairy Tales.

I utilized my German background and language ability to plan student trips and school exchanges. For one of the first outings, I escorted the entire sixth grade and their teachers on a train which followed the beautiful Rhine River to the West German capital of Bonn. First, we stopped in Bad Godesberg to visit the Beethoven Museum, after which the students ate a hearty lunch at the U.S. Embassy cafeteria and received a briefing by the American Ambassador, George C. McGee. Then we all boarded a bus to Cologne for a visit to its magnificent Gothic cathedral.

The group stayed overnight at the Bad Godesberg Youth Hostel. Our girls assisted with serving the food, cleaning the tables, and washing the dishes while the boys cleaned the floors. Afterwards, we viewed the impressive John F. Kennedy documentary, *Years of Lightning, Day of Drums*. The teachers and I had a challenging time getting everyone settled down to sleep in the dorm. But it was up early at six in the morning as the director of the youth hostel woke everyone with the ringing of a gong. After a delicious breakfast of Brötchen and hot chocolate, we visited the German Congress and were privileged to have a one-hour interview with Werner Marx, the CDU Congressman from the Kaiserslautern area.

I also arranged class visits to German schools in the area, as well as some one-on-one home exchanges with local families. This was beneficial because some American families seldom left the U.S. base and, therefore, had no appreciation of living in Germany. The Kaiserslautern Military Commander and the Lord Mayor of Kaiserslautern presented me with an award for my work in furthering German- American relations.

In the spring of 1967, Kaiserslautern #2's principal, Charles Jenkins, was offered and accepted a position in Washington, D.C. DoDDS Headquarters, so I was named "Acting Principal" for the remainder of the year.

When the complex was later assigned a supervising principal, Roger Prince, I received a promotion to GS 10 with the title of *Deputy Principal*. I was ecstatic when Mr. Prince informed me that I was to run the day-to-day operation of our school.

To celebrate my promotion and the end of the school year, Liz, Kathy, and I drove to northern Germany through the Harz Mountains, the Lueneburger Heide, to the exclusive German island of Sylt where many German movie stars had luxurious homes with thatched roofs, maintaining their original historic style. The three of us stayed with a local family in a German "bed-and-breakfast." It was a pleasure later that summer to accompany Roger and his wife Jane, a teacher at Landstuhl, in their search for a house and to acquaint them with the area. Before school, we two men made a trip to DoDDS headquarters in Karlsruhe to discuss staffing and share lunch with the Director, Dr. Joseph Mason. Mr. Prince proved to be an outstanding, caring boss who allowed me to run the school with a minimum of supervision.

In late spring of 1968, Liz and I were both accepted for graduate work at Miami University in Oxford, Ohio. DoDDS granted us each a year's leave of absence, and I received an Assistantship from the university requiring me to teach three courses in school law, both on the campus and in Dayton, Ohio.

Miami University 1968-69

Miami University had received a grant which allowed overseas administrators to matriculate for a year in order to complete the coursework for a new doctorate. I met fellow graduate students on a leave of absence from international schools in Russia, Greece, Israel, Poland, and Czechoslovakia. Dick Strickland, another DoDDS representative who was on leave as supervising principal of the Ramstein schools near Kaiserslautern, became my close friend.

I left Kaiserslautern for Miami immediately after school ended to attend the 1968 summer session and had to reside in a boiling dormitory without air conditioning. Since Miami was on a trimester system, I would eventually complete fifty graduate hours during my one-year leave-of-absence plus two summer sessions. Most of my time was spent in the underground stacks of the vast library, studying for classes and preparing for my teaching job—my small desk decorated with photos of Germany to keep me from becoming too homesick.

Eventually, Liz, Kathryn, and I moved into a small basement apartment in Oxford, Ohio, a far cry from our spacious military quarters in Kaiserslautern. Liz enjoyed her year as a faculty spouse. Kathryn was enrolled in an excellent preschool. We attended a few athletic events; however, I was very busy studying and Liz had the full-time job of being a parent besides taking classes for her Masters' degree.

Instructing the Ohio law course was a pleasure. Students were in their senior year and were eager to share their student teaching experiences. As part of our graduate work, they required us doctoral candidates to assist professors with research assignments and consulting work for neighboring school districts. Each Friday found us seated around tables in the Leadership Department, sharing lunch and interacting with our professors and other practicing school administrators on a variety of educational topics.

My advisor, Dr. Robert Simpson, an expert in educational law and international education, allowed me to write my dissertation on German education. John Trump, who also served on the local school board, taught me everything I needed to know about junior highs and middle schools—lessons which would come in handy when I administered the largest junior high school in Europe.

Assistant Dean of Education, Dr. Kenneth Glass, approved my taking additional course work each semester, enabling me to finish my course work before returning overseas.

Back to Kaiserslautern 1969-1972

After the 1969 summer session at Miami University, which consisted of research and writing the first chapter of the dissertation, our family returned to Kaiserslautern. Fortunately, we were again provided military quarters. It turned out to be a tough year because, in addition to my full-time job operating the school, I spent each Saturday and Sunday working on the dissertation and preparing for the orals and written doctoral finals. I successfully passed the latter at the end of October. Drs. Ralph Purdy and James Showkeir joined my advisory team in Oxford, which also included my former professor in counseling education, Dr. Gene Santavicca.

In late spring of 1970, Roger Prince accepted the position of superintendent of the Rhineland Pfalz schools and moved with his new staff into the annex next to our school. I was promoted to GS 11 and the position of principal of Kaiserslautern Elementary #2. Carl Gamberoni became my assistant principal.

That year, I made a lifelong friend in Art Kidder, a decorated Army veteran who was serving as the new School's Officer. Art and his wife and son lived in the small village of Trechtingshausen overlooking the Rhine, and Art went home only on weekends. After one particularly frustrating school day, he suggested an evening walk through the surrounding forest. With permission from Liz, our Wednesday ritual each week became a long walk in the countryside followed by a hearty meal in a local restaurant. Art was a brilliant walking partner because, like my music club friend, Jakob Becker, he could recognize every plant, tree, wild animal, and mushroom. Jakob and I took part in several *Volksmarches*, the initial one comprising a thirty-kilometer walk for a gold medal. I found these outings rejuvenating since I had literally studied each weekend for the past three years with little opportunity for physical exercise.

My final version of the dissertation was accepted by the committee and I was scheduled to defend it in Oxford on October 26, 1970. The flight from Germany to New York was uneventful.

However, just after everyone had boarded the plane from LaGuardia Airport to Cincinnati, the pilot announced, "We have received a bomb threat. Please leave everything behind and exit at once."

Determined not to be separated from my dissertation papers, I hid them under my coat, exited, and an hour later, took another flight to Cincinnati.

After my defense, the committee asked me to leave the room. In order to make the wait less stressful while the committee conferred, I was invited to speak to an undergraduate class about overseas schools. In the middle of my talk, Dr. Purdy entered the room. I knew the dissertation defense had gone well when he said, "*Doctor* Ellinger, you may come in now." It was a memorable moment. I drove to Cincinnati amidst a gorgeous sunset that matched my elated mood, back to my parents' home where Dad had a bottle of champagne waiting to toast my success.

Upon my return to Germany, the staff in Kaiserslautern presented me with a surprise breakfast and dressed me with a surgeon's outfit and face mask. They decorated the entire school building with congratulatory banners and posters. One student asked if I was going to work at the dispensary. I had to explain to the children that I was not the kind of doctor who gave shots.

Liz had been appointed superintendent of the Kaiserslautern Chapel Sunday School, which kept her extremely busy on weekends at the same time she was enrolled in a number of graduate courses which counted for the completion of her Masters' degree. I continued my previous practice of taking groups on field trips into the German community. One day I chaperoned 110 sixth graders to Rothenburg-ob-der-Tauber, the charming little walled town on the Romantic Road.

In early May, I escorted the entire faculty by train to Hamburg. I had arranged a good price with the German National Railroad, and we all had sleeper accommodations. We took several local sightseeing trips, and everything was going well until one of teachers asked, "Why aren't we going to the *Reeperbahn* nightlife area?" Against my better judgment, I agreed to take them there. The show was quite racy. Although I insisted that "the teachers made me do it," Sunday School Superintendent Liz didn't speak to me for a week.

As the school year 1970-71 drew to a close, several teachers became engaged. It was my job as their supervisor under Department of Defense regulations to interview them before approving and signing their marriage applications.

In school year 1972-1973 the staff consisted of thirty regular classroom teachers, three special education instructors, three special education assistants, specialists in music, art, physical education, and reading, a psychologist, a social worker, an instructional materials clerk, a tuition clerk, two secretaries, four German host nation teachers, an assistant principal and counselor: Margaret Heath Deanna Morgan, Lawanna Brown, Julia Kolat, Al Lipoff, Pat Matthias, Cathie Clark, Roberto Sanchez, Susan Dudley, Barbara Shirk, Lynn Peukert, Charlotte Potter, Ellie Rivelleno, Barbara Wright, Gertrud Ziegler, Ursula Kirsch, Doris Billington, Sharon Lester, and Fern Shands, to name a few.

When Dr. Mason phoned me personally at the end of the school year to offer me a GS 12 promotion to Principal, Frankfurt Junior High, it was initially a shock because I had expected a move to an elementary school. On the other hand, I was elated to be able to move to my old home town of Frankfurt. FJHS, the largest junior high in Europe, would be a challenging assignment for it had been in the news recently with bomb scares, teacher union unrest, and a bubble gym that frequently collapsed and blew away during the night.

I was invited to Frankfurt to meet with the Commander of the Hessen Military District and with my new superintendent, Herman Search, the man who had initially interviewed me for DoDDS in Cincinnati, and I combined the trip with a tour of my new school.

My visit to Frankfurt was not without its challenges. Earlier that week, a bomb, for which the *Bader Mainhofgang* claimed responsibility, had exploded in the Frankfurt Officers' Club, injuring several people. Just as I arrived at the junior high school, a bomb scare was called in, and everyone evacuated the building and proceeded to the Army gymnasium. Some students chanted, "We want to go home!" However, Assistant Principal Paul Papineau restored order.

After classes resumed, I dropped in on a few classrooms. Brian Byrnes, the Overseas Education Association's top negotiator, later told me that most teachers had a favorable impression of my visit. Before going home, I inquired at the government housing office where they assured me that my family would have an apartment by the middle of July, and I arranged for one of my teachers, Roberto Sanchez, who taught Spanish, to transfer from Kaiserslautern with me to Frankfurt Junior High.

The end-of-year faculty party in Kaiserslautern, where Liz and I had lived for nine years, was a bittersweet event. The faculty presented me with an international time clock and gave me lots of hugs. Kathryn ended her school year with a good report card and was sad to leave her friends. Liz received a sixth-grade teaching assignment at the huge Frankfurt Elementary #1 School.

[4]

Frankfurt Junior High
1972-1975

When Liz and I moved to Frankfurt in 1972, we were assigned military quarters in the Atterberry Housing area not too far from the junior high. On our first weekend there, little Kathy and I spent the afternoon by the Main River at a carnival. We rented a paddleboat, and as we enjoyed being on the water, I shared memories of my early years in this historic city.

The school year began with a successful teacher orientation, and Liz and I hosted a party for the faculty, which got us off to a good start. I was fortunate to have a terrific secretary, a former DoDDS Paris High student, Margie Kilpatrick, and a new assistant principal, Jo Kiley, who was an excellent disciplinarian. Assistant Paul Papineau, managed the numerous day-to-day tasks of keeping the school running smoothly.

The first week with the students went without a hitch. However, early in the year, there were several challenging issues that I had to overcome. During the prior year, students had thrown rocks down from the third floor at a greenhouse adjacent to the school, causing considerable damage and creating strained relations between the Americans and local residents. I met with the Frankfurt city administration officials and promised over a year's time to pay off the outstanding bill. To accomplish that meant selling gummy bears and candy from my office the entire year.

Next, a major racial incident occurred that set off a firestorm in this very volatile era of troubled race relations and could have caused the end of my short tenure at FJHS. Several black students ran into my office one day to tell me that a teacher had uttered a racial slur. Resolving it required a number of meetings with parents. Fortunately, we had a very strong minority studies program for both students and teachers. With the support of dynamic new black faculty members, the parents were convinced that DoDDS and the FJHS staff did not condone such behavior. Especially helpful was my good friend and counselor, Nelson Faddies, who had a significant influence on the students and was very active in the community. Throughout the year, the faculty and staff were always careful to involve black parents on school committees.

Obviously, student morale was an issue, intensified, perhaps, because the school was located on a closed campus surrounded by a wall. In addition, the Mid East oil crisis had eroded our funds for after school activity busses. To improve students' attitudes, my competent department chairs devised a special activity program that involved the majority of the student body. Each Friday afternoon, teachers offered students a choice of approximately twenty mini-courses, including intramural sports, anthropology, fencing, black culture, athletics, bachelor cooking, yoga, cosmetic secrets, model airplane construction, driver education, choral and instrumental music, and arts and crafts. This schedule also enabled students to meet in various school organizations. At the end of the year, by consensus, our Friday mini-course program had been an outstanding success.

Our efforts were rewarded when Lt. General Pearson, Frankfurt Military Community Commander, sent a letter complimenting us on the improvements made at the junior high.

We also received an excellent rating from a race relations follow-up inspection. I credit my talented faculty and department chairs, who improved student morale by upgrading the curriculum and expanding co-curricular offerings for the students.

I worked long hours at Frankfurt Junior High; however, Liz, Kathy, and I did take time for short weekend excursions in the vicinity of Frankfurt as well as returning to old haunts like Kaiserslautern, Weierhof, and Steinbach. I was able to hire my good friend, Art Kidder, formerly the schools' officer in Kaiserslautern, to work in my supply office. He and I continued our Wednesday nights out to include hearty German meals and a beer or two after invigorating walks in the vicinity. At the end of the school year, I got a much-needed rest by taking a family vacation in the vicinity of Marbella, Spain.

I recall several highlights to my years at FJHS. In the fall of 1972, I traveled to Berlin for some research. My primary goal in visiting East Berlin, behind the infamous Berlin Wall, was to get an initial impression of the school system in the communist city as gained from interviews with educators and from school textbooks.

I rode the underground train, not officially authorized, since U.S. government employees were required to cross only at Checkpoint Charlie. As I ascended the steep steps and reached the top, I suddenly faced an opening in the Wall. A hand reached out and a voice from within shouted, "Passport."

The official appeared surprised to see an American civilian. I asked him if it was all right to walk around the city and to take photographs. He replied, "*Natürlich*, of course, this is the Democratic Republic of Germany. You are free to roam around and take photos. The only restrictions apply to military subjects."

I had scheduled interviews at the *House of Teachers* or Department of Education where I received a thorough briefing, was given printed materials, and purchased several textbooks.

My interviews and subsequent research were later published in an article in the December 1981 issue of *The National Association of Secondary Principals Bulletin.*

I was told that the primary goal of education in East Germany was to instill socialism into each person, starting from the crib and continuing through adulthood. All students attended the ten-year comprehensive high school, in contrast to schools in West Germany where high-achieving students, as a result of a test, were placed in a university track starting in the fifth grade, while the remainder remained in the primary and middle schools. This distinction was touted by the East as the more democratic alternative for allowing all students the same opportunity to achieve.

As a history major, I was particularly interested in examining the GDR texts covering this subject and cited several in an article titled "School Textbooks in East Germany" that I wrote for the *Overseas Principal, Spring 1966-67 Issue,* a DoDDS Europe journal. From the fourth-grade text, *Birthday of the GDR,* I read the words of a First Speaker:

> "When I was born, war came to an end. We dwelled in ruins, and our shelter was riddled with bullet holes. During the day, the sun shone in. In the evening, the moon was our light. Mother did not know how she would feed us. There was no milk, and the bread was stale. She was concerned that I did not gain weight. But father said, 'These times will not last long. One day he will be as tall and maybe as fat as I was.' He laughed, but it did not seem funny to him. That was then in forty-five. When I was born our Republic was born."

> A Second Speaker was quoted:

"The first farmer and worker state. Our parents had lost so much during the war, but they still had the courage to start over. My father and many others went to work. They freed the land of rubble. They built machines, planted grain, and our Party assisted with everything. The West ignored us."

The third speaker speaks of new furniture, college education, paid vacations at the beach and what is to come.

Reading texts were aimed at realizing the goal of "educating the socialist man" as seen in these examples:

"Hans Juergen stands by the sentry box and speaks to the soldier, "What do you do here day in and out?"

"I am a soldier of the People's Army. Go ahead and play and have fun. I stand guard here throughout storms and snow to watch over and protect you."

"Are you aware of our most important goal? Success will come to whoever studies hardest. Whoever studies and works collectively doubles his strength. No one achieves the plan alone. Mother has come home late today. She remarks how clean the kitchen looks. Christel, Reiner, Klaus and Frank have cleaned it spic and span. No one achieves the plan alone. By the time you are grown, you will know exactly what is right. Then you will stand side by side in brigades, women and men. No one achieves the plan alone."

Back in Frankfurt, other highlights of the year include a faculty meeting I scheduled after school at the rotating Henniger Tower overlooking the area where my family's house was located in the suburb of Sachsenhausen. In addition to educational topics, I shared a brief history of my war years' experiences.

For a two-day curriculum conference at the Heppenheim youth hostel, on a scenic hill overlooking the *Odenwald* Mountains, I invited several curriculum coordinators from Karlsruhe to conduct workshops. While those attending worked hard during the two days, some partied late into the night, much to the distress of the youth hostel director.

The school had an outstanding choir and band directed by Ms. Yvonne Jaeger and Mr. Bob Romine, who were asked to perform throughout the surrounding area for both German and American organizations. They were invited to the German *Heimschule* in Weierhof by assistant principal Walter Lichti, our good friend. The German students, who heard only classical music at school, loved the modern tunes of the Sixties and Seventies performed by our students.

We managed to get through the first year without damage to the greenhouse and paid back all bills for the damage done in the past. No more selling of gummy bears! It was a good year.

At the beginning of SY 1973-74, the school hosted a Community Involvement Conference in the Taunus Mountains. We invited forty parents, students, and representatives from the community to discuss curriculum and instruction issues as well as to set educational priorities for the coming year. Involving parents in decision-making resulted in a successful start.

That year, under the able leadership of the English and Social Studies Department Chairs, Sara Ann Harroll and Zee Christopher, a new electives program was initiated for eighth and ninth graders. Instead of a year of *World History* and of *English I*, students were offered a choice among quarterly electives such as *History of the Middle East*, *History of Russia*, *Book Power*, *Newspaper Editing*, and *British Literature*, to name a few.

Frankfurt Junior High School was selected as the first Department of Defense junior high to undergo an evaluation by the North Central Accrediting Association. Dr. Dick Coss, European Deputy Director, led as the featured speaker at a two- day curriculum conference where the faculty rewrote the school's philosophy, developed descriptions of course objectives, and planned for the fall NCA visitation. Meanwhile, I visited Bonn High School to get pointers from their successful NCA evaluation, and computer scheduling was initiated under the able leadership of Phil Hokanson.

Towards the end of the school year, Liz and I learned that we would have to vacate our government quarters. After some searching, we found a spacious country house near Buedingen, in the little town of Limeshain-Hainchen. We made the big move into our country home surrounded by hundreds of boxes. It was a beautiful house with inside wood paneling, spacious rooms, and balconies on all sides that overlooked fields and forests surrounding our little village. The rural environment was a relaxing haven after a busy day at school in the city.

I decided to take a commuter train into Frankfurt to work. Since this train stopped in each little village en route to my final stop, Frankfurt—Bonames, it made for a long day. Although I could complete a number of reports on the way to Frankfurt, in the evening, on the way home, I frequently fell asleep and missed my stop. If it was too late to catch a return train, I would locate a *Gasthaus*, enjoy a beer with the locals, and call Liz to drive me home.

Under the direction of Anita Wander, drama and journalism teacher, students contributed a number of positive articles about life at FJHS to the local military publication and to the *Stars and Stripes*, which aided our public relations effort. Cathy Davies produced an outstanding slide show on all aspects of the school's program, which was widely used in presentations to parents and military commanders.

My final year at FJHS passed quickly and was made special by a visit from my parents. I also received a welcome Christmas present from the European Director, Dr. Mason, on December 21 when he offered me the principalship of the new five- million-dollar Hanau High School for SY 1975-76. The Hanau High complex was on a twenty- four-acre lot with football, baseball, and soccer fields, track, tennis courts, and even a three-hole golf course. Special labs included cosmetology, auto mechanics, and business.

I was elated because this gave me an opportunity to round out my administrative experience. There was little time to celebrate, although I made a quick visit to the new facility. Dr. Mason asked me to start in the spring overseeing the curriculum and course planning, so each week throughout the spring, I met with future Hanau Department Chairs to review curriculum issues. Helen Close, counselor, gathered course descriptions from various high schools to help prepare our own course of studies.

Immediately after the Christmas vacation, FJHS had its official visit by the North Central team, co-chaired by Al Kyrios, USDESEA Secondary Coordinator, and Dr. John Kemp, Chair of the Illinois North Central Committee. The team was extremely positive about all aspects of our program, and I felt it was beneficial for the Command and the parents to get an outside review and certification of our programs. Since lots of work had gone into the planning and write-ups, I was immensely proud of our faculty and the leadership of my deputy, Bill Yarbrough. I was pleased, also, to have my parents visit and attend the complementary out-briefing.

At the end of the year at FJHS, Liz and I were feted with a number of parties and farewell celebrations.

[5]

Hanau American High School
1975 - 1980

Hanau High School was built to shorten the commute of students living in Frankfurt High's outlying feeder communities which included Aschaffenburg, Babenhausen, Buedingen, Gelnhausen, and Hanau. Initially, the thought of transferring to the new school was a concern for many students, especially the juniors who had purchased FHS class rings and had fostered close ties and allegiance to Frankfurt High.

However, the students quickly caught the Hanau High Panther spirit. At the opening football game, the entire community came dressed in black and gold shirts. We defeated the always strong Brussels International School for our grid inaugural. Everyone was proud of our enthusiastic cheerleaders, and our women's drill team was already considered one of the best in Europe.

Ben Abrams, prep sports editor for *The Stars and Stripes*, wrote, "I visited Hanau last week and the school spirit is spectacular from Principal TomEllinger on down."

We were not so fortunate in the second game, with Baumholder, to which Kathy and I drove in our new black and gold VW. But as the season drew to a close, with Baumholder the leading team in the league, Hanau High was vindicated by defeating them in our final game, much to the joy of our fans. Deputy Principal, Leon

Rivers, his wife Anne, and Liz and I celebrated our victory at our favorite Chinese restaurant in Frankfurt.

Building and coordinating the various athletics programs and events was a major task, and I was fortunate to have Denny Lemmon as athletic director. He also coached our fall cross country team, starting practice during the heat of August with just seven young men and women. Each week, additional students joined until he had recruited approximately thirty enthusiastic young Panther runners. Coach Sandy Arbour was responsible for the girls' volleyball team, leading them in a successful first season. When I met with the community commanders of Aschaffenburg and Gelnhausen, both indicated that they were pleased with the initial start of the school and had received positive reports from parents.

The North Central Accreditation Team arrived in November to evaluate the school. Through a herculean effort on the part of our dedicated faculty, the numerous required reports were completed during the opening three months of classes. We passed successfully, and Hanau High became an accredited school.

Co-curricular activities, including Friday night dances, men's and women's basketball games, wrestling matches, and a myriad of other after school events consumed much of our time during this colder than usual winter season. Severe snow and ice made driving hazardous on the narrow country roads, so Liz, Kathryn, and I seldom arrived home before 9 pm.

During this inaugural year, the school was visited by numerous Congressmen and high-level military commanders. In early March, we hosted the District Drama and Forensic meet, adding 150 students to our school population. Most of the individual events were conducted in classrooms, giving valuable exposure to our students. Hanau High proudly captured second place.

The junior/senior prom was held in the spring on the boat *Mozart* which cruised down the Main River starting at the castle in Aschaffenburg. Students dressed in their finest enjoyed a moonlit night that featured a grand dinner, sightseeing, and dancing.

In June, parents and faculty proudly greeted Hanau's first graduating class as it marched to the strains of *Pomp and Circumstance* in the majestic royal residence of Phillipsruhe. Lieutenant General Kenneth Cooper, Deputy Commander-in Chief, U.S. Army Europe, gave the commencement address. The Junior ROTC Color Guard saluted the Class of 1976, and Colonel Charles J. Fiala, Commander of the 130th Engineer Brigade, presented the students with their diplomas.

The fall of 1976 again saw a flurry of activities including athletic events and banquets, dances, principals' meetings, and Open House, in addition to managing discipline and attempting to keep the teachers and the community happy.

Liz and I arranged a trip to Berlin at Thanksgiving. My primary purpose was to go to East Berlin where I had again arranged meetings with teachers and a principal at the *House of Teachers*. They shared materials on the East German education system which enabled me to publish an article in *The National Association of Secondary School Principals (NASSP) Bulletin*. After the meeting, Liz and I went on to visit the East Berlin Christmas market near the Alexanderplatz. I was thrilled to discover they served a favorite Saxon dish that my grandmother, who was born in the East, used to make for us as children. *Quarkkeulchen* are made from a dough containing mashed potatoes, cottage cheese (*quark*), eggs and flour, spiced with cinnamon or dotted with raisins, then baked as small pancakes in linseed oil. They are delicious served hot, with sugar, fruits, or other sweet side dishes. I also enjoyed a delicious bowl of pea soup with sausages for 1.20 East marks. We noted an interesting significance that the Christmas market in East Berlin featured only traditional and classical carols, unlike the secular music heard in the markets in West Berlin.

During spring break, Marv Kurtz, elementary coordinator, and I embarked on a memorable trip by train through East Germany. At our first stop, Leipzig, the capital of Saxony, we listened to an organ concert in St. Thomas Church, visited the town hall, strolled around town and shopped in a large department store. Our next stop was Frankfurt-on- the-Oder (River), situated on the Polish border. This town had the feel of the 1940's with buildings and churches still standing as empty shells—a result of World War II. We continued on by train south to Eisenhuettenstadt, which was billed as a model socialist city. Huge modern apartment complexes housed the people who worked in its sheet metal processing factories. Along the route, Marv and I participated in lively discussions with the locals who were more at ease openly criticizing their repressive regime while riding in the relative safety of private train compartments.

At the end of April, the PTSA held its annual bazaar made up of vendors from various parts of Germany. We opened the school campus to our German neighbors who loved to eat American hamburgers, hotdogs, and, especially, our ice cream. Unfortunately, as principal, I had to spend time in the dunking machine, an extremely unpleasant experience in the forty-degree weather. Our PTSA president, Judy Shepherd, worked diligently for weeks organizing this event which raised much needed dollars for our new scholarship fund.

The 1976-77 school year ended with a real highlight: Yvonne Jaeger, our talented choral music director, produced *The Sound of Music*, involving both students and faculty. Dr. Ron Downing, Deputy Director for the European Schools, gave the commencement speech.

In the fall of 1977, my good friend and able deputy, Leon Rivers, was promoted to Principal of Bad Kreuznach High School, and I was joined by Fran Smith, a knowledgeable educator with whom I had worked in the Kaiserslautern complex. Oakley McEachren, who had a good handle on school discipline, became my second assistant.

Our football team, under the able direction of Ed Driscoll, got off to a great start by defeating Berlin 49 - 0. In fact, during the first six games, no school scored a touchdown against us. We won the Silver Division championship by defeating Brussels International, 40 - 7. Unfortunately, the victory was marred by a pushing incident between rival spectators which led to an inquiry by the Supreme Allied Commander in Europe, General Alexander Haig. We won the Germany Class B championship in a squeaker, 7 - 6 against Augsburg. The cross-country team as well as the volleyball teams also won European championships, so the school celebrated with a huge athletic banquet.

Since I had taken no vacation the past summer, I decided to join Art Kidder in a one-week trip to Ireland in early October. After flying from Düsseldorf to Shannon International Airport, we rented a car and proceeded to Galway where we stayed at the Galway Ryan Hotel. The next day, we continued south along Ireland's magnificent west coast, past the Cliffs of Moher before stopping overnight at a bed and breakfast in Tralee. We thoroughly enjoyed the indescribable scenery of Dingle Peninsula where huge cliffs jut into the sea, and later drove around the scenic Ring of Kerry. Another night, we stayed in Killarney, situated on a beautiful lake surrounded by mountains. The hospitality, friendliness, and generosity of the Irish people made this trip a memorable one.

During the Christmas break, my family and I joined a number of other faculty members and their families for a ski vacation at the Hotel Kalkstein in Kirchhoff, Austria, a quaint little mountain village in Tyrol near St. Johann. Kathy skied downhill on the Steinplatte, Liz skied cross country, and I hiked the mountain trails.

By this time, our little black and gold VW bug had clocked so many miles commuting to athletic events throughout the country that its faithful Panther Spirit engine finally expired. I was fortunate that auto mechanics instructor, Ron Schmidt, and his students could replace the engine so that the Hanau Sports Machine continued to roll along. After championship football, volleyball, and cross-country seasons, we captured the All-Germany basketball championship for both men and women. The trophy case in our front lobby was filling up quickly.

Since I had heard nothing from my friend and superintendent Mr. Search regarding our seventh championship, I phoned him to ask what he thought of our successes. With his usual good-natured humor, he replied, "Ellinger, I don't give a darn how many athletic championships you win. I want to know how your reading program is going."

Spring of 1978 continued to be a busy time. I was elected president of the European Chapter of Phi Delta Kappa, the international education fraternity, which required me to make a number of trips to meet with the outgoing and new administrative boards planning strategy and programs for the upcoming year. Liz hosted the entire Hanau faculty for an end- of-the-year party attended by eighty teachers and staff. Fortunately, the weather held out.

During one of the early summer weekends, my family and I traveled to Wiesbaden to hear President Jimmy Carter speak. We stood close enough to the platform to see the First Lady Rosalynn Carter and their daughter, Amy, as well. Other dignitaries that accompanied them included German Chancellor Helmut Schmidt and Secretary of State Cyrus Vance.

Later in the summer, I attended a seminar on East and West German education in Berlin. Speakers included professors from the Free University of Berlin, from the Max Planck Research Center, and from the Berlin Senate. One morning session featured a lecture on East German education, presented in the *House of Teachers* in East Berlin. In addition, we participants enjoyed a number of sightseeing tours and an evening reception with West Berlin educators.

A highlight of School Year 1978-79 was a huge Phi Delta Kappa meeting hosted by Liz and me in January. Liz did a fabulous job organizing this function which was attended by over 300 teachers from throughout northern Europe. Dr. Cardinale, DoDDS Director, gave an excellent speech on the new reorganization of the school system. Hanau parents and teachers outdid themselves preparing their delicious favorite dishes for the attendees.

Later that evening, Liz and I relaxed and unwound at our home in Hainchen with Dr. Cardinale, who would spend the night with us. It was then he mentioned that he thought I had been in Germany a long time. "Perhaps you should think about an assignment in the Far East," he suggested.

In the fall of 1979, sixteen new faculty members joined the staff at Hanau High. We continued receiving parent accolades. Curriculum reviews by district and headquarters staff were positive. Graduates received a number of valuable and prestigious college scholarships. Course offerings were expanded under the direction of department chairs Peggy and Chuck Messner, Bob Prinz, Phil Hokanson, Brian Byrnes, Paul Ristow, Judy Timpano, Bob Leach, and Ralph Simpson.

The Hanau Panthers defeated Heidelberg for the Red Division football crown with stars Morris Jelks and Howard Easley leading the charge. Coach Driscoll, who had cruised through the Silver Division in 1977 with a perfect 8-0 record, ran his overall winning streak to fifteen. During half time of the Homecoming Game, I escorted the lovely Freshman Princess, Kathryn Ellinger, onto the football field. We later captured the All-Germany championship against Kaiserslautern, 21 - 18 in a thriller.

The new Germany North director, Dr. Blackstead, and a number of curriculum liaisons arrived from the Pacific Region in Wiesbaden. Dr. Blackstead introduced his staff and shared his vision of greater decision-making authority for principals, to include matters of personnel and budget. I eventually invited each of the new district coordinators to our school and had the pleasure of getting to know many of them personally.

As second semester began in January, 1980, I didn't realize that it would be my last in Hanau. Dr. Blackstead invited me to spend six weeks beginning in April on a team recruiting new DoDDS teachers from the United States.

I thoroughly enjoyed the recruiting trip although it was an extensive time to be away from my school. The team, made up of administrators from all districts throughout DoDDS, initially met in the Washington Headquarters Office to examine teacher application files. I was assigned to interview teachers in Baltimore, Boston, Philadelphia, and Cincinnati.

Baltimore proved to be challenging because many of the teachers attending the interviews already earned higher salaries than DoDDS offered. I recruited a few teachers who drove in from outlying areas, among them, Gay Marek, who would, some twenty years later, become my Language Arts liaison in the Mediterranean District. Ray Guastini, principal of Mannheim

Elementary, and I were more successful in Boston where we recruited on the nearby air base.

In Philadelphia, I was interrupted during an interview and told that I had a telephone call from Okinawa. The Pacific Chief of Education, Joseph Larkin, calling on behalf of Pacific Director, Edward Killin, offered me the position of District Superintendent of Korea. After finishing my interviews for the day, I walked to the nearest bookstore to purchase a guide on Korea. I was so extremely excited that I could barely sleep that night. Cincinnati remained as the final stop on my recruitment tour, so I was able to stay with my parents and share the news.

My return to Hanau was bittersweet. When my supply clerk, Richard Ganz, met me at the Frankfurt Airport, he insisted that I come directly to the school although I was dead tired. Escorting me to the multi-purpose room, he flung wide the doors. "Welcome back!" the entire faculty and student body shouted. The celebration continued, led by the cheerleaders with music from the band and choir.

After the party ended, Liz and Kathy joined me in the car for the drive home, greeting me with stony silence. When they could contain their emotions no longer, both exclaimed, "How could you do this to us?"

Although we had discussed the possibility of going to Korea, we hadn't resolved some of the issues. Liz would have to take a leave of absence from DoDDS because she was not allowed to teach where I was superintendent. Kathy would have to leave all of her friends, including her boyfriend Wayne, and Hanau High, the school she loved.

Meanwhile, Al Willendrup and his Korean wife invited us over for a delicious Korean meal and a slide show, as did counselor Pete Price who had worked in Pusan. Cafeteria worker Jeannie Simmons, a gracious Korean-American lady, also invited us to dinner and briefed us on some of the local customs. Jeannie would remain at Hanau where I would see her on June 5, 2008 when I presented remarks at the closing of Hanau High and its military community.

The 1979-80 school year drew to a close with the senior prom being held at nearby Ronneberg castle. Many students stated that they would miss me, which made me feel very happy yet nostalgic at the same time. At commencement, Dr. Robert Lundgren, Germany North Deputy Director, gave an inspiring address to the graduating seniors, and I received a standing ovation from parents and students as well as a silver plaque from the senior class, presented by their sponsor, Hal Bardach.

When my parents came to visit in late June, I escorted them to southern Germany and Austria, leaving most of the difficult work of packing to poor Liz.

[6]

First Decade in Korea

So, after eighteen years with DoDDS in Germany, I departed for the Far East with a promotion to District Superintendent of Schools in Korea. En route, I attended the worldwide DoDDS administrators' conference in Boston, which provided a perfect opportunity to meet many of the liaison staff from the Okinawa Pacific Region as well as my principals assigned to the Korea District.

I finally arrived at Kimpo International Airport, Korea, on Saturday, August 3, 1980. My business manager, Eileen Stansbury, and the school's faithful Korean driver, Mr. Chon, met me, and soon after, I was indoctrinated into the teeming traffic of Korea's capital city. Mr. Chon skillfully manipulated the van in and out, dodging cars, trucks, bicycles, and pedestrians as we made our way to the Yongsan Army Post, a quiet, leafy military housing area located in the middle of the huge concrete city of Seoul.

I had preceded my family to this assignment to ensure they would have a roof over their heads when they arrived. Initially, I lived in a single, compact room in the Bachelor Officers' Quarters, supplied with a bed, refrigerator, sink, desk, and a large fan. Fortunately, there were numerous clubs and restaurants on post, serving excellent food to include European, American, Chinese, and Korean fare, for relatively inexpensive prices.

Eileen put me on a rigorous work schedule that commenced the following day, Sunday. Although I was still exhausted from jet lag after the long fourteen-hour flight, I realized she had good intentions and wanted me to meet with as many of my local administrators and staff as early as possible. She entrusted me with a number of briefing folders on all aspects of school operations to include the budget and personnel statistics.

Early in the week I was scheduled for a fifteen-minute appointment with the American USFK Commander, General Wickham, in the vast headquarters building referred to as the "White House." Entering and walking through the building, I passed several military guards and representatives of the various countries that made up the United Nations Command. The general, seated next to a huge map of the Korean peninsula, was extremely welcoming and informative about our military mission.

Next followed a whirlwind tour throughout the peninsula to visit the schools in my district. I distinctly remember my initial trip to Taegu, Korea's third largest city. Mr. Chon drove me to the K-16 Airbase outside Seoul at the crack of dawn one early September morning, where I boarded a small C-12 aircraft. The flight to Taegu traversed mountainous terrain whose various air currents played havoc with that little bird. I looked down at rugged mountain peaks as the plane wobbled back and forth, up and down, and worried just what would happen if we were forced to make an emergency landing. Soon rice paddies and level ground appeared, and we came in for a smooth landing executed by our able and experienced Army pilot.

Lowell Jacobson and Jim Hayden, principals from both Taegu schools, were at the airport to meet me in a staff car which took us to Camp Walker. Each invited me to dinner during my stay, so I was able to meet their lovely wives. Upon entering the Hayden home, Kyoko, who is Japanese, led me to an easy chair, handed me a scotch, and gave me the Stars and Stripes to peruse while she continued fixing a delicious meal. Jake's wife, Margaret, was just as welcoming. During my visit, I was introduced to the staff of each school and immediately worked on remembering names, a practice which served me well in my years as superintendent.

Leaving Taegu, I boarded the 125-kilometers- an-hour "blue train" on a scenic ride through pastoral fields and rice paddies southward to Pusan on the coast. I was met at the station by principal, Chet Karpowitz. His driver ably negotiated the harrowing traffic to Camp Hialeah, which had once served as a racetrack and now housed the school and military families. Chet and his wife, Joanne, hosted a party for me and their staff, serving delicious Korean fare. A courtesy visit with the local commander and classrooms visits were on my next day's schedule.

I was driven by a staff car to Chinhae, nestled in a tranquil coastal mountain region with gorgeous scenery. Principal Ed Atterberry and his lovely wife, Becky, greeted me and invited me to dinner in their spacious Navy home. Ed introduced me to the Base Commander and to the small school staff the next day before escorting me on a tour of the city.

To reach the elementary school on Osan Air Base required an hour and a half driving south from Seoul, depending on the density of traffic on the major freeway connecting the capital city to Pusan. Fritzie Osner, a chemistry Ph.D., was the administrator of the one-room schoolhouse built by the Red Horse Air Force Engineering Group. All grades, K-6, met in this large building, using only a few bookshelves for classroom dividers. At Osan, as in our other schools, approximately sixty percent of the students were Korean-American. A number of the military men requested consecutive tours to Korea and married local spouses. Their children, hearing mostly Korean at home, were for the most part studious, well-behaved and had a great work ethic.

When Liz and Kathy arrived in late August, our wonderful sponsors, Kay and Ed Davies, invited us over for dinner on a number of occasions and helped us in all aspects of getting adjusted. They guided us on walking tours to Seoul's downtown tourist attractions, the palaces and the ancient city gates plus endless colorful markets featuring all varieties of clothing, shoes, household goods, numerous items required for daily existence as well as fresh meats, fish, rice, noodles, cabbage, and other vegetables.

Besides relaxing during the three-day Labor Day weekend, Liz, Kathy, and I toured the Korean Folk Village, viewing the large outdoor museum's many exhibits of restored buildings from the past. We attended a performance of traditional Korean dancers who, wearing elegant silk gowns, gracefully swirled colorful silk scarves and painted fans. Together, we sat on cushions on the floor at low tables to sample the local cuisine, practicing our skill with chopsticks.

The following weekend we boarded a bus for the "Demilitarized Zone" at Panmunjom, on the border between North and South Korea. After a thorough briefing in the American facility, we were escorted on foot by tall, robust American soldiers to the small metal building in the center of the United Nations zone where negotiations take place between North and South. Stern-looking North Korean soldiers stared us down from outside their facilities while their loudspeakers blared anti-U.S. propaganda.

Liz and Kathy and I temporarily moved into a leased military housing area, RGH, across the Han River until the quarters on Yongsan we had requested became available. Late evening rides from Yongsan to our quarters were sometimes extremely stressful, for Seoul was under military control and we had to ensure that we were home before curfew. Kathy adjusted well to her new high school and was pleased to be selected to the volleyball team, which enabled her many opportunities to travel around Korea, Japan and Okinawa.

The quarterly superintendents' conferences were conducted on Okinawa, headquarters for the Pacific Schools, and were attended by the superintendents from the Philippines, Korea, Okinawa, and Japan, in addition to the chiefs of the various headquarters departments of Personnel, Logistics, and Education. My transportation to Okinawa involved riding backwards on a C-141 military transport plane which stopped at various bases in Korea to unload or pick up passengers and cargo. Hours later, I finally arrived at the sprawling Kadena Air Base.

Dr. Killin, our supervisor, hosted a party in his spacious military quarters overlooking the Pacific Ocean. Okinawa was extremely hot and humid, just as I remembered it. But I noted some changes. The main north-south highway which was only a dirt road when I was on Okinawa in 1960 now consisted of a six-lane highway lined with palm trees. Kadena High School Principal John Shaver was kind enough to drive me to my old BOQ, where I had spent my first year at Machinato.

Subsequent trips over the years to Okinawa were always highlighted by dinner invitations to the homes of good friends on the Pacific staff to include Pat and Dick Saddlemire, Karen and Rick Carpenter, Sally and Eric Hohenthal, Carolsue and Don Fenwick, Ellen and 'Smitty' Reeves, Deputy Director, Arlyn and Howard Sweeney, and Masako and Dennis Ward. Special friend and former Chinhae principal Stan Hays always met me at the airport and showed me the fabulous new Japanese resorts along the coast, along with other local landmarks.

Early in the school year, my staff and I planned Dr. Killin's first visit to Korea. Since his rank was equivalent to a three-star general, we were fortunate to obtain designated private military transportation for him, thereby enabling us to visit all the

Korean schools in record time. Riding in the army helicopters lifting Dr. Killin and me above the rugged mountain ranges, I felt like we were taking part in the television series *Mash*.

Liz and I appreciated the sunny autumn weather of Korea, marred only by the strong Seoul pollution, after the cloudy years in Germany. However, winter arrived with a vengeance, and we often experienced days when the wind chill factor was ten to twenty below zero Fahrenheit.

The highlight of the New Year, 1981, was the annual administrators' conference, held the third week of January in Baguio, Philippines. I departed icy Seoul, Korea and landed three hours later in tropical, eighty-three-degree Manila. The following morning, I spent a few relaxing hours by the pool at the Holiday Inn Hotel overlooking Manila Bay before boarding a bus in the late afternoon bound for Clark Air Force Base, the largest U.S. military base in the world.

I spent two days in Superintendent Don Ellis's office, along with the other headquarters division chiefs, discussing "Merit Promotion" papers for teachers and administrators who had applied for promotion. The first evening, we were all invited to Dixie and Chuck Di Massio's beautiful house off base. I discovered that folks in the Philippines lived royally. Many had a maid as well as a gardener who tended lawns that featured lush vegetation with tropical trees, palms, shrubs, and flowers.

The following evening, Al Lipoff, formerly one of my very capable teachers in Kaiserslautern who was currently serving as Business Manager for DoDDS Philippines, hosted me at the Clark AFB Officers' Club. It was great to see Al and reminisce after all those years.

The conference commenced the next day at Camp John Hay, one of the most famous resorts in the Philippines, located on the outskirts of Baguio. To reach it, we rode in a bus up steep, narrow, treacherous roads. The site consisted of vacation cabins available for American soldiers and families on R&R, great conference facilities, and the big attraction—a very hilly but scenic nine-hole golf course. I enjoyed a stimulating week listening to various speakers while feasting on American and Filipino fare and soaking in the sun.

Meanwhile, back in Korea, Liz obtained a teaching position at Seoul International School in midyear and was enrolled in two evening courses. She enjoyed her terrific students from the various international businesses and embassies. However, the school had practically no heat, so she sometimes wore three layers of clothing and arrived home at night to soak her feet in a tub of warm water. A few years later, Headmaster Ed Adams would build a very modern, Korean-style school structure.

In the spring, Educators' Day, a once-a-year highlight, allowed some three hundred teachers from the various DoDDS and private schools throughout Korea to share educational strategies and methods. At this annual conference, held in the Seoul International School, teachers presented workshops in areas of their expertise. A number of outside speakers included curriculum coordinators from Okinawa, as well as professors who taught for the various American universities represented on the post at Yongsan.

At the end of my first year in Korea, I received the Thumbs Up Award for SY 1980-81 which read: "Tom Ellinger, Education Program Administrator (EPA)-Korea, for Outstanding Assistance in Quality Education and Teacher Rights to DoDDS Employees in Korea." Although I was proud of the award, it probably did not endear me to my good boss, Ed Killin, who frequently scolded me for not being tough enough. Fortunately, I had an excellent relationship with country teacher representative, Ofelia Robles, and, although we did not agree on every issue, we considered student welfare above all other concerns. I had also been fortunate to recruit our friend, Kay Davies, for the position of secretary. Kay, who had prior experience as an executive secretary working for various superintendents on Okinawa, was invariably able to pacify angry parents before I got on the line—an invaluable asset in running my office. A second valuable addition to the staff this year was Seoul High School teacher, Steve Schrupp, who was promoted to the position of business manager and who reorganized the fiscal and logistics functions into a more efficient operation.

Decision Time

January 1982 was decision time regarding our family plans. Kathryn was a senior at Seoul High School and would be graduating in June. Liz's two- year Leave of Absence from Germany would be up in June, and still regulations prohibited her from working for me in Korea. I was offered a number of principal positions, both in the Pacific and in Germany. However, both Liz and I hoped that eventually a change in the regulation would allow us to work in the same location while I remained in my superintendent's position.

In February, I was invited on a North Central Accreditation visit to Iwakuni, Marine Corps Air Station, Japan. Flying first on Northwest Airlines to Fukuoka, I then boarded the 225-kilometer-an-hour "bullet train" to Hiroshima, where the first atomic bomb was dropped on August 6, 1945. High school Principal Bill Ryskamp, who would later become my business manager, met me at the airport. The team worked diligently during the week, getting up at four to write reports and attending late night discussion meetings. On the weekend, the elementary principal, Renee Fajardo, escorted us to Hiroshima where we visited the Peace Park, the Memorial Museum, and the Eternal Flame commemorating the victims of the attack. In the Peace Park, a tiny Japanese lady asked to have her photo taken with me. Her friends giggled at our height difference, but I was touched that all animosities were temporarily forgotten after such a tragic event.

In late spring, Liz, Kathryn, and I were invited to join a tour paid for by the Korean government led by Ed Adams, Headmaster of Seoul International, who had published in excess of twenty books and was extremely knowledgeable in all aspects of Korean history and culture. In addition to visiting the iron and steel works in Pohang and a shipbuilding facility in Ulson on the coast, we toured Kwang Ju, capital city of the ancient Silla kingdom, now a tourist attraction considered a national treasure.

The end of the semester came too soon for all of us. Kathy graduated seventh in her class of seventy-five seniors and won a $2,000 scholarship. Ambassador Richard Walker delivered the commencement address, and I was able to hand Kathy her diploma on stage. It was a stressful time for our family as we planned to go separate ways. Liz, still not allowed by DoDDS to teach in a district where I was superintendent, decided to return to Germany and reclaim her position. She was assigned to Bad Kreuznach as the Gifted and Talented coordinator for the Bad Kreuznach, Mainz, and Dexheim schools. Kathy would attend the University of Colorado in Boulder, and I would remain in Korea and move into a small BOQ on Yongsan Post.

Bachelor Year 1982-1983

I was henceforth a geographical bachelor. Before leaving, Liz fixed up my little quarters with some of our furniture and even planted flowers outside the room, giving me great comfort. Fortunately, people felt sorry for this *de facto* bachelor and issued me a number of dinner invitations.

Most evenings in August, I rode to the airport with the driver, Chon, to meet the incoming teachers who were assigned to our various school locations throughout Korea. Those destined to schools in the south were housed overnight in a local hotel and, the following day, taken to the train station to board the Blue Train. The stop in Taegu lasted only three minutes, so we always hoped teachers had time to get off with all their suitcases. Not all succeeded.

Liz and I both looked forward to our Christmas rendezvous in Germany. For the initial segment of my 30,000 mile around the world trip, I took a slow C-130 flight to Okinawa. In addition to regional meetings, I attended a number of pre-holiday parties prior to making the long flight to Frankfurt. Liz met me at Frankfurt International in her newly purchased Volvo for the drive to Bad Kreuznach. Since her school was still in session, I took a train to my old high school, Hanau, the following day. On the ride back, I was so overcome by jet lag that I slept right through the scheduled stop at Bad Kreuznach, not waking up until Koblenz. Liz had planned a candlelight dinner that night, and having my chair at the table empty didn't go over too well after not seeing each other since summer. Other than that, we had a great reunion.

Before returning to Korea, I flew to the United States to attend my parents' 50th wedding anniversary celebration in Cincinnati on December 31, 1982.

Reunited 1983-1984

In the fall of 1983, when Liz became eligible for a transfer to Okinawa by agreeing to pay her own transportation including the shipment of household goods, she received a position at Kadena Elementary School. From there, she was able to get a space available flight to Korea, so for a few days, we had the whole family together while Kathy joined us from Colorado.

Exciting news from headquarters! DoDDS announced a regulation change which now allowed teachers married to superintendents to work in the same country/district as their spouses. So, a few weeks after the start of the school year, Liz was reassigned to a fourth-grade class at Seoul Elementary School. We moved into a tiny BOQ room and were put on a waiting list for family quarters.

Meanwhile, since I had worked all summer and had some vacation time coming, I signed up with a Korean social agency to take Korean orphans to families in Detroit in October. Prior to the trip, I attended a two-hour information session, which included training in making formula and changing diapers. The day of the flight, I was escorted to the agency and put in charge of six tiny babies along with a Korean woman who spoke no English. By carrying one baby in each arm and having one strapped to our backs, my Korean partner and I boarded the Northwest plane to Detroit. We were given four seats in the front of the tourist section for the six infants. One or two babies were always screaming, much to the consternation of the remaining passengers who were trying to rest. I continually carried infants up and down the aisles in my attempt to get them to sleep. After thirteen exhausting hours, we were finally able to deliver the babies into the welcoming arms of their new parents in Detroit. Before returning to Korea, I enjoyed a short visit with my parents in Cincinnati.

The fall semester of 1983 was particularly hectic and troublesome. I received a call claiming that the Pusan principal, who had served in Korea for sixteen years, had confiscated approximately $500,000 of government funds during this time period, primarily from tuition money. A team of Headquarters personnel was dispatched to investigate, along with the CID and local auditors. They inspected the budgets of our office and of the remaining Korea schools, which fortunately were in top shape. I will never forget flying to Pusan and addressing the principal, staff, and community. I replaced the principal with my very able district Education Generalist, Betty Taira, who did a marvelous job in keeping the school afloat for the remainder of the year. If it had not been for my supportive USFK./UN Commander, General Robert Sennewald, my administrators, teachers, and supervisor on Okinawa, I would have experienced a great deal more difficulty getting through this very stressful time.

What a joy to welcome the arrival of spring in Korea that year as the first forsythia and azalea bushes appeared in bloom on our post! The chapel choir I sang with prepared an Easter cantata directed by the outstanding choir director, Joan Miller, a Yale graduate who had sung professionally throughout the United States. We performed two concerts in the chapel before touring isolated military outposts near the border to sing for the troops.

As a "thank you" for our support of the JROTC program, I was fortunate to be invited, along with my high school administrators, on a trip to Hawaii, paid by the Army. We stayed at the Reef Hotel on Waikiki. It felt so good to relax after this very stressful year, enjoying late afternoon drinks on our hotel balcony and evening dinners at the Hale Koa or the Hawaiian Hilton Hotel. During the day, we visited a number of military bases to review their training operations, and I was impressed with the professional attitude of our soldiers. We also saw a missile site, an area for jungle warfare preparation, and a helicopter simulator.

The Seoul American High School JROTC program, founded by COL Paul Snyder and CSM Al Braswell in 1981 and later ably administered by LT COL Dave Menig and LT COL Don Hedgpath, was without a doubt the best in the world of the overseas dependents' schools. Our students throughout the years received numerous academy appointments, honors, and ROTC scholarships. This "Honors with Distinction" program was later expanded to Taegu and Pusan and became the pride of the United States Army in Korea. In September of 1995, the first Air Force JROTC program was established in Osan.

Honors

In the fall of 1984, Seoul American High under the direction of Principal Ed Davies, was nominated as one of 143 schools in the United States to be designated as a Department of Education Model School. We learned in October that Seoul American made the final cut. The recognition ceremony was conducted in December by Assistant Secretary of Defense, Marybel Batjer, who presented the staff with a huge banner and plaque. Ed, who had meanwhile transferred to Okinawa, returned for the ceremony and received a standing ovation. Nancy Hill, instructor at Seoul American, received the Outstanding Math Teacher Award, and Sally Yoshida was named Outstanding Science Teacher. Our exceptional Seoul High art teacher, Michael O'Brien, later received the prestigious DoDEA Teacher of the Year Award, and Betty Noone and John Blom were named Distinguished Elementary Principals.

That same year, the Army provided DoDDS with a small facility for the new Pyontaek School on Camp Humphreys, and our very able Mr. Gorwood coordinated with Korean contractors to renovate the building. We advertised and recruited two local military dependents to teach in the school and opened with approximately fifty students. Special Education Coordinator Paul Finkbeiner volunteered as the first principal. Being a distance runner, he appreciated the rural atmosphere which allowed him to jog on the winding roads between Pyontaek and his Osan home.

I was fortunate to recruit Ed Atterberry, former Chinhae principal, as business manager. He was extremely effective at supervising the budget, personnel, and logistics functions. Marcia Mason arrived from Japan as special education coordinator. Being well versed in all aspects of special education, curriculum and instruction, she also served as our Education Generalist. Five years later, she would marry the talented principal of Osan and later Seoul, John Blom, on the very day the Wall went down in Berlin. District computer coordinator, Ray Paulson, followed by Nancy Alberti in the early eighties, established our technology programs in the various schools, starting with installing office computers to accomplish such tasks as scheduling and enabling teachers to input grades electronically.

During the Eighties, Korean university students became ever more volatile in their anti- government demonstrations; however, the riots, which looked dangerous on U.S. national television, were confined to the areas surrounding the university campuses and were usually dispersed in a couple of hours.

In the spring of 1987, the country again faced huge anti-government demonstrations as hundreds of Korean students marched to the railroad station in Seoul to board trains bound for the North Korean border. Americans who lived off base faced huge traffic jams and were occasionally affected by the pepper gas. I won't soon forget the last day of school. The Korean bus drivers went out on strike just as we were closing. After some strong "convincing" laced with threats of dismissal, they agreed to take our students home. On a sad note, my very efficient secretary for the past four years, Lesley Smith, departed with her family to the United States.

Phil Hokanson, former Frankfurt and Hanau teacher, joined my staff as computer coordinator at the start of SY 1987/88. Although Seoul was a constant buzz of activity, making it such an exciting place to live, one did not have to worry about crime in this metropolis of ten million people. Consequently, Phil, CSM Al Braswell, and I often strolled through the city in the evenings, negotiating steep hills, touring quaint paths and alleyways, and passing busy fruit, vegetable, and meat markets and mom and pop stores which stayed open until 11 p.m.

During the winter of 1987-88, I taught a University of Southern California course in Kunsan, an unaccompanied Air Force base in southwestern Korea. It felt like the coldest place on earth, with strong gales and snow blowing in from the sea. At the initial meeting, I found it difficult to involve the students, the majority of which were fighter pilots, in any discussion about schools and education. I learned later that they had attended an all-night party before class, but they were extremely bright men and women who became enthusiastic class participants.

For Christmas vacation, computer coordinator Phil Hokanson and I traveled to Kuala Lumpur and Singapore. This colorful city combined ultra-modern buildings and avenues with ancient structures and narrow alleys, so we booked a morning tour to include a number of mosques, temples, monuments, and markets. We visited both the Chinese and the Indian areas to enjoy their markets with vendors selling exotic foods and handicrafts. On Christmas Day, we toured a rubber plantation, a tin mine, a scorpion farm, a batik fabric-dyeing factory, and a Malay village built on stilts.

Located two degrees from the Equator, Singapore reminded Phil and me of a tropical New York City with manicured lawns, gardens, and parks. We walked to the 101-year-old Raffles Hotel, where Kipling, Michener and many other great writers have stayed, to experience the exotic British Empire setting that featured ceiling fans, manicured gardens, restaurants, and bars. There, we enjoyed a cool "Singapore Sling" and attended a floor show depicting Singapore's past.

In the afternoon, we joined a city sight-seeing tour of the Botanical and Tiger Balm Gardens. Although we consumed the majority of our meals in tiny noodle shops, savoring such specialties as roast duck, pork liver, partridge, and wonton shrimp soup, we did succumb to a couple of Big Macs on the way. One evening, we ventured on a stroll into Chinatown, one of the few quaint areas left in the city. Narrow alleys and numerous fruit and vegetable stalls were nestled in a concentrated area amid modern skyscrapers. I found it amazing to see that so many diverse peoples and cultures could exist harmoniously side by side.

The fall opening of SY 1988-89 was an exciting time for everyone in Korea anticipating the upcoming Olympics. I rearranged the school schedules to start at 7 a.m. and close at 1 p.m. so that teachers, parents, and students could attend these special events. Due to threats from the North, many potential international visitors canceled their flights, and we Americans stationed in Korea were able to purchase a number of tickets to various events at the last minute.

Pacific Director Jerry Bloom visited our district in mid-October. I was happy to see him since he had been at Frankfurt High while I was serving as principal of Hanau. After a stint as Director of the Mediterranean, he had served as Interim Director in Washington. Now Jerry and his able Chief of Education, Lee Davis, brought new energy to the Pacific district. Teachers appreciated his instituting a Pacific transfer program that allowed those teachers in isolated areas to request assignments to Okinawa. After a reception at the Hartell House, he addressed our Korea principals' meeting. The following day, he and I boarded a helicopter for Pyongtaek where he addressed parents.

We flew back by chopper to Seoul over tree tops in their glorious fall foliage and were picked up by staff car for a meeting with the Assistant Chief of Staff of the Eighth Army. In the afternoon, we met with the Assistant Secretary of Defense for Manpower, Grant Green, who was visiting Korea. He had listened to some concerns about schools from parents in Germany; however, he fortunately heard only compliments from the commanders here.

Winter break, 1988, found Liz and me at the elegant Tanjung Aru Beach Hotel in Kota Kinabalu, Malaysia. Located in a picturesque setting on an unspoiled beach in the China Sea, it featured numerous indoor and outdoor restaurants and a vast swimming pool. White-clad waiters brought exotic drinks and delicious Malaysian and American dishes to our poolside chairs. Evening dinners consisted of buffets on the spacious lawns to include shrimp, lobster, white fish wrapped in banana leaves, a variety of vegetables, and delicious desserts. In the midst of such an array of Oriental culinary treats, we were delighted to find a reminder of Christmases Past: *Weihnachtsstollen*, the traditional German Christmas cake.

Early March 1989, Liz and I were invited, along with approximately 300 Embassy and Eighth Army personnel, to a reception for President and Mrs. George H. W. Bush at a small U.S. Air Base on the outskirts of Seoul. I was permitted to escort three Seoul Elementary and three Seoul High school students. After waiting approximately an hour in a special hall, we heard the announcement: "Ladies and Gentlemen, the President of the United States, Mrs. Bush, and Secretary of State, James Baker." The president thanked us for our dedicated service to our country. After his five-minute address, he walked into the crowd, shaking hands with guests to include our students.

A few weeks later, I lost my dear father on March twenty-third, the day of my mother's birthday. He was 89 years old and had suffered from various ailments including prostate cancer since 1985. Notified that he was failing, I was able to get home to Cincinnati and spend the last few days with him.

German Reunification - 1989 to 1990

I had the privilege of returning to my native Germany at Christmas, 1989, to witness firsthand the euphoric celebration of freedom, the opening of the wall in Berlin, and the celebrations of people up and down the border joining hands for the first time since 1945. Just a month earlier, following the jubilant night of November 9 when the news of the East-West German border opening was heralded, Bild Zeitung headlines captured the feelings of many people: "Good Morning, Germany, It is Beautiful Awakening!" It had been a beautiful evening with tears of joy flowing on both sides of the wall. East Germans streamed across the border, surrounded by cheering West Berliners. Most could hardly believe their good fortunes. Many had thrown only an overcoat over their nightclothes to breathe the air of freedom—to just have a look—to see if it were actually true that one could go happily from one Germany to the other.

Recalling again that news pronouncement, "Good Morning, Germany! You can hope again. Your divided worlds are coming together. What a glorious awakening," I find it is difficult to describe my feelings while standing in the Frankfurt and Munich train stations, meeting trains from the East German cities of Leipzig and Dresden crowded with joyous people bearing suitcases exactly like the ones my mother and I had carried during WWII. They were overwhelmed by the abundance and quality of goods in the stores, the availability of unlimited food items, the absence of long lines, and the warm welcome they received. East Germans in their little "put-put" cars on the Autobahns received waves from all who passed.

It is a long way from Seoul to Berlin; however, the distance would not deter me from going back several months later for the historic unification celebrations in this exuberant capital on October 3, 1990. While the Lufthansa aircraft spanned the miles across the Asian continent, I pondered the miraculous march toward German unity which had begun with the opening of the border last November. As our jet made its final approach from Frankfurt to Berlin's Tegel Airport, I tried to concentrate on this truly remarkable event which no one would have predicted even a year ago.

The festival of unity between the *Unter den Linden Strasse* and the *Alexanderplatz*, attended by hundreds of thousands of people from all over the world, resonated with music from Allied and local bands. Shortly before midnight, the famous Liberty Bell rang on the Day of Reunification, followed by the raising of the German flag in front of the famous *Reichstag* Building to the strains of the national anthem. A joyous, exuberant crowd cheered this historic occasion.

After the ceremony, I drove my rental car into the former East Germany to Goethe's home town of Weimar, to the Buchenwald concentration camp where my father had been interned over sixty years before, then onward to the historic cities of Dresden, Leipzig, and Pottsdam, to include my grandmother's former home in Glauchau.

[7]

Final Years in Korea

When the world entered its final decade of the twentieth century, our DoDDS students in Korea were in frequent contact with other students in a number of U.S. and international locations. Through satellite telecommunications and the new email, they received almost daily messages from teachers and students at Berlin American High School, keeping us informed on German reunification and East Berlin news. Berlin students from both sides related to Korea as a divided nation and were especially interested in South and North Korean relations.

As a result of an introduction by our supportive Yongsan Commander, COL Joseph Simino, I established a close friendship with the director of Moonil High School, one of the largest private high schools and colleges in Seoul, a Dr. Kim Young-sil. On my first visit, I was ushered into his office for a cup of ginseng tea and conversation where he told me that, when he was a young student, an American missionary had noted his academic potential and provided him with money and a ticket to attend a missionary school in Japan. Afterwards, Dr. Kim escorted me on a tour of the school and college. As we walked through the halls, every student gave us a bow. Upon our entering the teacher's lounge, every instructor rose and bowed. In the soccer stadium, the air reverberated from the rousing cheer of a thousand students as we passed. Dr. Kim was especially proud of his library and study hall. He told me that one third of the 3700 students, who finish school at 5 p.m. and go home for dinner, return to the supervised study hall to continue their homework or to receive tutorials from seven to 10 p.m.

South Africa

In the summer of 1990, I flew to England to spend a few days being royally entertained by DoDDS friends, Dick and Beverly Strickland, Tony and JoEllen Carmone, and Lowell and Grace Peiper. Lowell and I ventured on a walk in the English countryside near the country estate of Margaret Thatcher.

After this brief stopover, I joined my good friend, Command Sergeant Major Al Braswell, at Heathrow Airport in London on July 27, and, with some trepidation due to reports of sporadic violence at our destination, we departed Heathrow on the thirteen-hour flight to Johannesburg, South Africa.

CSM Braswell had meticulously prepared for this trip since February, when news of Nelson Mandela's release from prison was announced. I sat next to a charming lady, originally from Scotland, married to an Afrikaner, who provided a great overview of the country.

Shortly after our arrival, Al and I boarded a plane for Cape Town where we stayed at the five-star Cape Town Sun Hotel with its magnificent view of Table Mountain. The city is one of the most scenic in the world, with breathtaking views of the Cape of Good Hope and of Cape Point where the Atlantic and Indian Oceans meet. In the evening, we attended a special service at Bishop Tutu's cathedral and heard a magnificent concert by a local boys' choir.

Leaving Cape Town, we flew back to Johannesburg, a modern, bustling city partially surrounded by man-made mountains of waste rock. Suburban homes owned by white residents were tightly secured, and their inhabitants lived behind large brick walls and thick gates.

Through an arrangement by my seatmate on South African Airways, Al and I were able to visit the huge, sprawling township of Soweto, home to approximately two million black residents. A gentleman who builds low-cost homes for local residents gave us a tour of the area. His construction foreman invited us to lunch with his family in their home. Outside, chickens, livestock, and poorly dressed children crowded the dirt roads as the wind unmercifully enveloped them with dust.

In Johannesburg, Al and I boarded a bus northbound for Kruger National Park. Besides viewing the exciting wildlife in its natural habitat, we treasured our evening walks under the magnificent star-filled sky highlighted by the Southern Cross.

Liz and I would remain in Korea until the end of School Year 1995-96. I volunteered with the USO at the military's beautiful new MWR hotel on Yongsan, the Dragon Hill Lodge, every Saturday afternoon from 1991 to 1996, an activity that involved sharing information on post facilities and downtown points of interest for newcomers or visitors to the country. The hotel served as an excellent meeting place for teachers, parents, and commanders from down country who visited Seoul for a weekend of rest and relaxation. I cherish fond memories of holiday decorations in the spacious lounges, Korean and American choirs and pianists performing around the white grand piano in the lobby, premier dining in a choice of three restaurants, and the cacophony of sounds and voices resonating in this international atmosphere.

In the aftermath of the 1991 eruption of Mt. Pinatubo in the Philippines, the location of our yearly January administrators' conferences was moved to Tokyo at the New Sanno Hotel, which maintained spacious conference rooms and excellent restaurants and shops. We enjoyed walking around in the relative safety of Tokyo at night alongside thousands of people hurrying home from shopping or work. I was given the privilege of opening the initial conference by introducing our new Director, Dr. John Stremple, who with his wife, Myrna, visited the Korea schools the following week. The closure of the schools in the Philippines also resulted in a number of educators being transferred to Korea, to include Principal of the Year, Ron Warner, who subsequently built a close-knit team of talented and dedicated educators at Osan. Two new dynamic administrators joined the Korea staff, Ruthie Morgan at the reopened Pyongtaek School and Diane Bell at Taegu. Both had an immediate positive influence on their schools and communities. Bruce Taft and later, Ben Briggs at Seoul High School and John Blom at Seoul Elementary, with their staffs, continued the tradition of providing high academic standards at their institutions.

Each summer break for several years, CSM Al Braswell and I would meet in Miami Beach before venturing on a one-week trip to a Latin American country. In 1991, we visited Costa Rica, and in the ensuing years, we explored Ecuador, Colombia, Bolivia, Guatemala, Brazil, El Salvador, and Nicaragua.

While I was away on an official trip in January 1992, attending a conference in Germany in Eastern Europe, the superintendent's office in Seoul was destroyed by fire. Someone from Central Texas University with offices on the first floor had left space heaters on unattended, and our little wooden structure burned quickly to the ground. My very brave secretary, Cathie Jennings, mother of *Jeopardy* winner, Ken Jennings, climbed up to our office on the partially demolished second floor to rescue a few valuables, including my government bonds which I had foolishly locked in my desk. I lost thirty years of DoDDS paraphernalia and many valuable books. The Post Commander provided us with a temporary office until August when we moved into the former JROTC building at Seoul High School.

An even greater loss was the passing away of my dear mother on March 4, 1992, from a massive heart attack, thereby ending my thirty years of writing letters home. She was a heroic lady who saved my life and that of my brother, Steve, my grandmother, and herself on a number of occasions during the Second World War.

Publications

In the early Nineties, I co-authored two articles on education in South Korea. I had been extremely impressed with the work ethic of the Korean students and their fervent drive to succeed. The first was written with Dr. Deborah Carlson, Assistant Principal of Pusan School, in response to South Korean students' scoring first on a world-wide standardized math test and appeared in the June 1990 issue of the *Foreign Service Journal*.

In a second article, published in the April1997 issue of *Phi Delta Kappan* and titled "Placing Education on Top of the Family Agenda," Gerry Beckham and I spoke to the role of the family and of rigorous curriculum as integral to the achievements of Korean students.

The days are long for Korean students. During the day, poorly heated classrooms house an average of 40 to 50 students sitting in well-worn desks arranged in long, straight rows; evening classes are conducted in equally cold rooms that seat 200 students hunched over tiny wooden desks, many of which are of 1920 to 1940 vintage. After study hall, a Korean student's day is still not over; many view an educational television channel or work on homework assignments from 7:30 p.m. until midnight. Others attend evening *hak gwan,* private institutes in which they receive supplementary academic lessons.

Private tutoring is an important aspect of Korean education. Educated people from all age groups, from retired people to university students, share their skills as tutors, earning supplemental income in the process. In the preschool and kindergarten years, students receive tutoring in such subjects as art and music. In elementary school, they receive private instruction in English, writing Korean, and music. While in the early years these sessions are more fun, once a student enters middle school, the lessons become a virtual component of his or her education.

Like everything else in Korea, education matters. Koreans view education as they view other aspects of life: a process of winning and losing. The family emphasis on educational achievement is so strong that it has been dubbed "education mania."

The driving force behind this education mania is the Korean mother, who has the primary responsibility for the education of her children. When a student enters school, his or her mother ensures that the youngster completes his homework, provides help with instruction in such subjects as reading and writing, and oversees the child's attendance at special after-school classes that supplement academics or provide enrichment. Once the student reaches middle school, the mother schedules every minute of her child's after-school time at special academies and institutes or in private tutoring.

To guarantee that she is well acquainted with her child's teacher, a Korean mother visits the school four and five times a year. During one of these visits, she will undoubtedly agree to the use of corporal punishment on her child if that is deemed necessary by the child's teacher, and she will promise to support the teacher if the child requires some prodding to complete assignments.

Both public and private high schools must follow the national curriculum. There are special schools for the most accomplished students in science, foreign languages, music, and art. Admission to these schools is extremely competitive, and students must meet rigorous entrance requirements to be accepted by them.

To summarize, Korean children attend school for a longer day than American students as well as spending an additional two hours in the evening in supervised study halls. They endure a rigorous secondary school schedule with no electives. A supplementary tutorial emphasizes mathematics. Finally, Korean students do not have the distractions of the many extra-curricular activities which are a part of a typical American student's schedule.

Professional changes

During one of our world-wide superintendents' conferences, DoDDS's new director, Dr. Lillian Gonzales, announced a major reorganization moving additional resources to district offices to ensure proximity to the schools. In Korea, we added new staff to include Assistant Superintendent Jane Ware, School Improvement and Staff Development liaisons Karen Arceneau and Ellie Micklos, Evaluation and NCA Coordinator David Doss, and Budget Officer Earl King. Four subject matter specialists joined the district: Connie Hellge, language arts, Tim Connors, science, Carol Babcock, math, and Dennis Rozzi, social studies. Our staff already included Bill Ryskamp, Business Manager, Marcia Blom, Special Education, Vivian Worth and Pat Gnida, Technologists. This system worked well and allowed principals and teachers to receive timely assistance.

Because of ever-increasing traffic between Seoul and our outlying areas at Osan Air Force Base and Camp Humphreys, the Korean government agreed to build us a new high school in Osan so students would not spend long hours commuting to Seoul High. On September 28, 1995, I participated in the Ribbon Cutting Ceremony at Osan High with Korean education and construction dignitaries, Brigadier General Foglesong, USAF, DoDDS-Pacific Interim Superintendent Dr. Richard Cawley, Principal James Szoka, and student body and faculty.

November 3, 1995, was another proud day for DoDDS Korea. I escorted the wife of the Chairman of the Joint Chiefs of Staff, Mrs. Joan Shalikashvili, and Mrs. Luck, the wife of our Korea Commander-in-chief Gary Luck, to the beautiful new Osan High School. We were greeted by Air Force JROTC cadets wearing brand new uniforms and ushered into the cafeteria where a reception of parents, teachers, and students awaited us with music from the school's jazz band. Members of the student body guided us through the new building and described the community partnership in Osan by telling how parents assisted in preparation for the new school to include setting core values and assembling furniture.

As she became acquainted with the duties of her position, our new director, Dr. Gonzales, expressed concern about the number of years some of us had worked in the same overseas location. She initiated a five-year rotation plan for principals and superintendents. Since I was serving my 15th year in Korea, it was no surprise that on her visit to Seoul in 1995, she indicated I would have a new assignment. At the end of February, she offered me the Turkey/ Spain/ Islands District, which extended from the Azores to Bahrain, an expanse of 6,200 miles. I happily accepted, and Liz was fortunate to receive an assignment as Teacher of the

Gifted and Talented in Adana, Turkey, where my headquarters were located.

The spring of 1996, as we made preparations for our move to the far side of the world, was an exciting and memorable time of parties and farewells. A large number of the Seoul and Osan faculties, in addition to administrators and teachers from other locations throughout the country, attended the magnificent farewell party given me by my office staff at the Dragon Hill Lodge Hotel. Four-star General Gary Luck presented me with the Superior Civilian Service Award and sat with Liz and me at the head table. It was a glorious evening. My successes in Korea would not have been possible without superb teacher, administrator, and military support.

[8]

Turkey - Spain - Islands District
1996-2001

Adana, Turkey, a sprawling metropolis of approximately 1.3 million people, is situated in an agricultural area one hour's drive from the Mediterranean Sea in the shadow of the 12,000 ft. Taurus Mountains. Liz and I arrived there on a sizzling one-hundred-degree evening on August 3, 1996. The ride from the airport to the İnçirlik Air Base through teeming traffic, barely missing pedestrians as they scurried across the dusty roads, hundreds of small minibuses and yellow taxis repeatedly honking their horns and zigzagging back and forth, made for a thrilling beginning.

It took some getting used to our new surroundings. Early memories include the Muezzin calling the faithful to prayer, reminding us that we had arrived in the exotic Middle East. During my initial courtesy visit with the Wing Commander, I stated that, as superintendent of schools in Korea, my wife and I had lived on base and I was considered "key and essential." Without hesitation, he countered, "Doc, you don't fly a plane and don't carry a gun. You are not key and essential here."

Living on the economy turned out to be a blessing because the apartments downtown were larger than base housing, and we had the unique opportunity to experience the local culture first hand. We rented a spacious apartment in a sixteen-story high rise structure in town, overlooking the turquoise Seyhan River, with a courtyard of palm trees, banana groves, and a huge swimming pool.

The superintendent's office was located on Inçirlik Air Base, a staging area for NATO sorties over Northern Iraq. Our staff supervised the Dependents Schools in Turkey, Spain, Bahrain, and the Azores, making it the largest geographic district in DoDDS, covering 6200 miles, which, if interposed on a map of the United States, covered a distance from Miami to Honolulu.

The staff welcomed Liz and me with a traditional Turkish breakfast at the Officers' Club. Mary Davis, the Assistant Superintendent; Joe Robinson, Art and Humanities, who later became a successful principal of the Ankara School; John Bunch, Business Manager; Bonnie Butt, Language Arts; Kim Purcell and Patti McNaughton, Math; Tim Connors, Science; George Grantham, Social Studies; Debbie Frick, Budget; Kathleen Pleshaw, Dorie Parsons, and Vivian Worth, Technology; and Gul Inal, our Turkish secretary, all worked diligently to provide a quality program for our 7000 students.

Retiring superintendent, Edna Brower, and her husband, Ted, hosted a spectacular party for Liz and me at their beautiful lake house on the outskirts of Adana. She accompanied me on my first trips to the schools in Ankara and Izmir.

The capital, Ankara, is one of the most modern cities in the country with wide streets and a European atmosphere. The DoDDS school population is composed of students from embassies of over forty-five foreign countries, in addition to the local Air Force dependents. A memorable event in Ankara was their yearly international festival where students, dressed in the traditional costumes of their native countries, participated in a fashion parade, and, along with their parents, shared cultural and culinary highlights of their homeland. On this first trip, we were hosted by Principal Bob Marble, who would later become my Chief of Staff at Inçirlik. We received a mission briefing from the Major General, who was in charge of the U.S. Air Force in Turkey. At the end of the school year, he hosted the senior graduation exercises followed by a grand garden party at his residence.

From Ankara, Edna and I flew on Turkish Air to Izmir. Assistant Principal, Bob Seider, met our plane, then escorted us through the school, which was in an old tobacco warehouse one block from the Aegean Sea. Both elementary and high schools were located in unmarked buildings, protected only by concrete barriers and Turkish guards. A later building that we leased and renovated in a nearby area was likewise a constant concern to our security officials and military commanders, who felt that the building was in jeopardy of a possible terrorist attack.

Stars and Stripes reported, "To approach the new school located in one of Izmir's grittier neighborhoods, one must dodge the teeming traffic, pass junk stores, *doner kebab* stands, and a shop selling spare parts for Russian-made Minsk motorcycles." Crossing a street meant taking your life in your own hands. The school, however, had a talented staff and a dynamic principal, Cathy Magni, who offered the students a superb education.

Otherwise, Izmir was considered an excellent assignment due to its location on the Aegean and close proximity to the Turkish Riviera. I fondly recall evenings sitting with friends in wonderful sidewalk fish restaurants overlooking the calm seas of the Aegean. A pleasurable after school conference meant spending time on one of numerous small boats anchored to the shore, lazily rocking back and forth in the sunset, enjoying an Efes beer and a dish of delicious calamari.

In mid-August, I attended our district administrators' conference in Istanbul, my first opportunity to meet with the principals in the district and to hear the well-planned curriculum presentations by my staff. The Kalyan Hotel, site for all district staff development and principals' meetings, was located on the Marmara Sea. We could watch ships, tugs, and steamers headed for various Mediterranean ports from our balconies and the dining room veranda. The hotel was within walking distance of the Blue Mosque and the Grand Bazaar, so we always looked forward to meeting in this, the world's most exotic city.

Later in September, I traveled on Turkish Airlines to Frankfurt, Germany and by train to Wiesbaden for a European Superintendents' meeting with DoDDS Director, Dr. John Davis. He introduced us to his regional staff, and we discussed educational and budget priorities for the upcoming school year. He was a super, supportive boss throughout his DoDDS-Europe tenure.

Bahrain

At the end of the conference, I departed Frankfurt International for my first visit to Bahrain in the Persian Gulf, with a brief stop in Abu Dhabi. Principal Carl Albrecht, an exceptional administrator who was highly regarded by the local government, parents, teachers, and students, met my plane and drove me to the Gulf Hotel, which overlooked the Persian Gulf and a grand mosque. This hotel with its many world class international restaurants would be my "home away from home" whenever I visited Bahrain. I especially loved the English breakfast buffet featuring eggs benedict, ham and bacon, and a vast array of Arabic and European entrées.

The following morning, Carl introduced me to a select group of student leaders who escorted me through the school and its environs. I was extremely impressed by all I saw until the students guided me on a walk outside the main building through deep desert sand to various annexes. The temperature was a stifling 113 degrees! When we passed the grand school swimming pool, I wished I had brought my bathing suit. On subsequent visits, these same students always personally greeted me by name and inquired if they could be of assistance.

The Bahrain School, a model educational establishment, was built by the Amir, and the majority of its students are non-military, although there is a sizable US Navy population. Fifty different nationalities are represented. Students attend classes on Saturday and Sunday and observe the Moslem holy days on Thursday and Friday. Most are enrolled in the academically challenging International Baccalaureate, and all non-military students are required to take Arabic. Ninety-two percent of the graduates will attend prestigious four-year colleges in Europe, the United States, and Canada. I noted that when I was introduced to Advisory Chair Dr. Dhafer Ahmed Alumran, who occupied a high-level position in the Bahrain Ministry of Foreign Affairs, he was dressed in his traditional Arab robes. During my tenure as superintendent, I had ample opportunity to visit all classrooms and was extremely impressed with the level of expertise of this diverse faculty, staff, and students.

Next, Admiral Charles Moore invited me for a briefing in his office where I learned that the American military mission in Bahrain is in support of the Admiral of the 5th Fleet and encompasses a huge geographic territory extending to the southern tip of Africa.

For the evening, the dynamic head of the Arabic Department, Adrine Katchadurian, invited me along with Admiral Charles

Moore and the U.S. Ambassador, David Ransom, to her lovely home where we socialized with various sheiks, five ambassadors, and some local businessmen. It was a memorable evening.

On the last night of my initial visit to Bahrain, Carl and his lovely wife, Lucia, hosted a reception for the school staff and me at the "Stars and Bars" Bar in the Gulf Hotel.

My journey back to Turkey was, by contrast, rather unpleasant. During the long layover in the airport at Riyadh, Saudi Arabia, I was not particularly welcomed by the stern customs officials who insisted, although I was only a transit passenger, on seeing my Saudi visa, which I did not have. Then, the flight to Adana, scheduled to depart at four in the morning, was crowded with Moslem pilgrims returning from their Hajj to the holy city of Mecca.

However, on a subsequent visit, I had the good fortune to meet with the Amir of Bahrain. His Highness, Shaik Isa Bin Sulman Al Khalifi, greeted me in one of his official reception halls before we were joined by the Prime Minister, the Minister of Justice, and numerous additional sheiks and dignitaries, many of whom were graduates of our school. The Amir was a very warm, pleasant gentleman and great friend of the United States. He conversed with me about his hopes for world and Middle Eastern peace and reiterated his pride and support for the school.

The evening of my visit, I was called to the front desk of the hotel where a well-dressed gentleman waited to hand me a small white package. "A gift from the Amir," he said. I thanked him and took the package up to my room to open. There in the box lay a gold Rolex watch probably worth in the neighborhood of $14,000. Unfortunately, due to government regulations involving gifts, I had to send the watch to our headquarters office in Arlington.

The Azores, Portugal

Flying to visit our school at Lajes Field in the Azores, 800 miles west of the coast of Portugal in the mid-Atlantic, was a lengthy adventure that involved layovers in Istanbul, Paris or Madrid, and Lisbon. In fact, it often required overnights in Lisbon on both ends of the journey, allowing me fabulous sightseeing walks and a good meal in the Portuguese capital city. Air Portugal made the three-hour flight into Lajes Field a pleasant journey, especially if winds over the ocean were calm.

The Azores are a cluster of nine volcanic islands, with our school located on Terceira. Emerald green pastures trimmed with stone fences, quaint villages, old men riding on donkeys, exotic plants, and spectacular ocean scenes make these islands a scenic wonderland. The weather on my first visit was perfect as a slight breeze came in from the Atlantic.

DoDDS operates a small elementary and a high school there with approximately 500 students. During my first visit, I met with commanders, parents, and advisory committees and addressed the faculty. My initial official meetings with the Overseas Federation of Teachers (OFT) union representatives and spokesperson, Ernie Lehman, were conducted in a modern off-base hotel overlooking the ocean. To show good faith, we switched sides half way through the negotiations so that both management and union would have a panoramic view of the Atlantic. The meeting atmosphere for the most part was very cordial.

High school principal, Gil Fernandes, and his lovely wife, Shirley Anne, who is a gourmet cook, invited me to dinner. On subsequent visits, I shared memorable evenings with teacher friends, John and Jayne Bockman in their gorgeous home on the ocean, with Susan and Hal Wippel, and with Mary Wisdom and Dan Dittmeier. Tom and Anna Birch escorted me on scenic walks around the island. In the late nineties, the new high school principal, Jerry Ashby, and his lovely wife, Molly, with their three daughters, often hosted me in their beautiful home situated on a hill overlooking the Atlantic. I was fortunate to recruit Missy Klopfer as the new elementary principal. Both Jerry and Missy were outstanding administrators and were highly respected by parents, students, and commanders.

Rota and Sevilla, Spain

I always looked forward to my stay at the sprawling Naval Base at Rota, Spain. Endless days of sun and blue skies, palm trees, tropical vegetation and proximity to the Atlantic made this an ideal assignment. On all my visits, the Captain and his staff treated me to a VIP room in the very comfortable military hotel. Gene Perillo and Barbara Rudometkin were the administrators on my initial visit. In ensuing years, principals Gary Edsall and E. B. Stafford were strong leaders who both enjoyed outstanding community and command support.

Both faculties at Rota normally hosted a dinner for me at the affectionately named "Chicken in the Dirt" restaurant featuring delicious local cuisine. The Rota staff had many talented educators who were always anxious to invite me into their classrooms and homes. I fondly recall sunset parties at Tom and Sheila McCready's home in the little village of Puerto, sipping the local red wine while listening to Neil Young on their rooftop terrace overlooking the Atlantic, then later wandering through the town, stopping at little bars to savor more wine and watch the flamenco dancers in their colorful costumes. Karen and Dennis

Hurst were other frequent hosts whose daughter Kira had taught at Seoul American High School.

The elementary school featured a very sought-after Spanish immersion program and, later, an FLES or Foreign Language in the Elementary School program. Also, Rota's Reading Recovery Program was a model initiative which was later exported to other schools in the district.

Rosemary Letenoff, the Sevilla principal, drove me from Rota to Moron Air Base, an hour from Sevilla, where we operate a small forty student K-8 school, ably negotiating the narrow, winding roads. On Sunday afternoon, she and her two teachers escorted me into the historic town of Sevilla for a couple of hours of sightseeing in the picturesque city with its world-famous cathedral. We enjoyed a light afternoon lunch at a quaint restaurant, serenaded by local musicians. On Monday, I visited the school, met with the commander and, in the afternoon, rode back to Rota. I have fond memories of later visits to Sevilla, hosted by principals Ed Tyner and Steve Hain and Steve's lovely teacher spouse, Cindy. Transportation officer Mike Stanley drove me on numerous occasions between my schools in Sevilla and Rota.

Inçirlik Schools, Turkey

Sam Menniti served as principal of Inçirlik High School in Adana,Turkey and later became my assistant superintendent in the Mediterranean District. Shortly after his promotion to district superintendent of Korea in early 2009, he contacted leukemia and passed away in the fall of 2009. He will always be remembered as one of the best all-time educators in the world of DoDDS. Jean Waddell was the capable elementary principal at Inçirlik. Since our district office was eventually located in the elementary school, I treasured walking up and down the halls when I was in town, greeting our wonderful teachers with a "good morning" and visiting their classrooms. Fran Austin and Debbie Folmer, both outstanding principals, served the school during my last years in the Mediterranean. I was pleased to recruit Peggy Bullion at the high school. Walter Ulrich served as her assistant and was later promoted to principal.

Due to the frequent travel around my 6200-mile district, I was often too exhausted to do much touring on weekends. However, I had the wonderful fortune of visiting some major biblical and tourist sites in conjunction with my work. One-half hour south of Adana is the city of Tarsus, the birthplace of the Apostle Paul, who returned here after his conversion. It was a special experience to walk these ancient Roman roads to the church and the well where Paul started his preaching ministry.

Two hours' drive from Adana and 12 miles from the Syrian border lies the city of Antioch or Antakya, the starting point of Paul's missionary journey and the place where the gospel of Matthew was probably written. We often took a number of our North Central Accreditation teams to visit an ancient cave that tradition claims was dug by St. Peter himself and is the site where he started the first Christian church.

On the other side of Turkey, our school in Izmir was located an hour and a half from the ancient site of Ephesus near the Aegean Sea, considered as the best-preserved city of the classical world. Saint Paul lived and preached here for three years around 50 AD, and afterwards wrote his letters to the Ephesians. I had frequent opportunities to visit this magnificent site, especially during high school commencement exercises when the seniors from Izmir graduated in front of the façade of the ancient library, built by a Roman citizen in memory of his father. A house nearby is believed by many Catholics and Muslims to be the place where the Virgin Mary spent her last years, according to the 1812 vision of a bedridden nun.

Liz and I considered Cappadocia, located between Adana and Ankara, as one of our favorite locations. Volcanic eruptions, erosions, and thousands of years of wind have formed a nature wonderland of unique chimney rocks. Early Christians, seeking to escape persecution, settled here and lived in underground cities for long periods of time, building provision rooms, ventilation chimneys, wine producing places, churches, abbeys, water wells, toilets, and meeting rooms. Some rooms were connected by tunnels so narrow that only one person could pass through.

Since Cappadocia was only a three-hour bus ride from Adana, we held a number of district meetings here, including one of our very successful parent leadership sessions. We invited parent representatives from locations throughout our district, including commanders and their spouses, to join in discussing various educational and curriculum issues. Our subject area liaisons briefed parents on the latest content developments in language arts, math, science, and social studies. Because the hotels, some built in the style of the surrounding landscape, usually had colorful carpet shops nearby, I am certain the parents were impressed, not only by our professional staff but also with the once-in-a-lifetime cultural experiences we offered them.

My staff conducted an administrators' meeting in the resort town of Antalya, whose narrow streets lined with small houses, restaurants, and hotels lead down to its beautifully restored harbor filled with excursion boats, fishing vessels, and yachts. Many German and other European visitors enjoy this tourist paradise each year. We could book our hotel during the off season and travel there by bus for $20.00 a person along the narrow, winding road bordering the Mediterranean Sea.

Other district meetings were conducted in Istanbul—to me, the most exotic city in the world. East meets West here, where the continents of Europe and Asia come together. I never tired of this exciting city. Our conference hotel was within walking distance of many of the tourist attractions to include the Blue Mosque, which dominates the Istanbul skyline.

After a day of meetings, some of us would climb the steep hill, lined on both sides with ancient- looking wooden structures, to our favorite shopping place in the world, the Grand Bazaar. Our visitors, parents, teachers, and educational consultants especially enjoyed this world class shopping experience where they might haggle for hours with local merchants. The owners gladly hauled down scores of carpets, explaining their origin, always hoping to conclude a sale. Rows and rows of merchandise line this huge covered market comprising some sixty-five covered streets crammed with approximately 4000 tiny shops, restaurants, and cafes. For the social studies teachers and other more serious sightseers, our district social studies coordinator, George Grantham, an expert on Byzantine culture, hosted workshops and escorted tours to the many famous sites throughout this historic city.

Adana, Turkey

I thoroughly enjoyed my time in Adana. Our downtown apartment location made it possible to walk to various places of interest in the old and new sections of town. Wandering down narrow alleys and streets with teeming crowds and exotic sounds and aromas helped me forget the everyday stresses of my job.

Old Adana, I thought, was especially appealing. Frequently, a local man wanting to practice his English would approach me, inviting me to his or his friend's carpet shop. The appetizing aroma of fresh bread bought by the locals hurrying home for supper or roasted chestnuts burning over coal, the strong exhaust of vehicles racing down the crowded narrow roads, the haunting call to prayer from the minarets of the local mosque, all made for an unforgettable day. New Adana, on the other hand, had wide palm-lined streets with exclusive shops and a gold bazaar.

I won't forget riding the minibuses or *dolmus* to work on the Inçirlik Base. I had to change buses a number of times, not an easy task since I was non- conversant in Turkish. However, they were an inexpensive way to travel and relieved my initial anxieties of driving. Blaring, pulsating Middle Eastern music, strong body odors, cigarette fumes, near collisions with pedestrians, taxis, and other vehicles, nevertheless, made for a memorable ride.

Late afternoon or evening walks along the scenic Seyhan River became a part of my routine when in town. I was often joined by friend and neighbor Gary Boue, a teacher at Inçirlik High, who carried a big pole which he hoped would be our defense against any rabid, stray dogs and/or potential terrorists we might encounter along the way. Seriously, I had attended a number of security briefings on the activities of terrorists, including the Kurdish rebel group PKK, and our DODEA Safety and Security Officer in Arlington, Virginia had warned me that our particular location was one of the most dangerous in the overseas system. Nevertheless, I personally—perhaps foolishly—never felt uneasy or fearful on any of my wanderings through the local countryside.

Gary Boue recalls our evening adventures, writing:

> *"Myths and reports of people found drowned in the Seyhan River were rampant in the urban legends of Adana. Traversing the street from our apartments to our walking path was treacherous. We had to watch each other's backs attempting to cross what was*

the equivalent to a Turkish freeway boulevard. We wasted no time and stepped up the pace. We crossed on top of the Seyhan Dam to the opposite side of the river and walked upstream to the mini San Francisco Golden Bridge, whose structured beams were outlined with tiny lights. Vendors selling various assortments of nuts and pistachios, freshly squeezed orange juice and sweet desserts, lined the banks."

Outside the base in İncirlik, in what they called the "alley," were numerous shops selling carpets, gold, jewelry, purses, shoes, and copperware. The most famous was *Big John's,* well-known by every military and civilian wife worldwide. Big John and his partner, Small, a retired Air Force Master Sergeant, carried a wide variety of Middle Eastern wares and antiques in the shop and annually hosted our educators at parties in their complex.

I found the local cuisine especially appealing. The specialty was Adana kebab, minced lamb mixed with hot pepper, squeezed onto a flat skewer and then charcoal grilled. It is served with sliced purple onions dusted with fiery paprika and parsley and a side dish of delicious flat bread served hot that I liked to spread with butter and honey. Appetizers, or mezes, which included delicious spiced cheeses, yoghurt with cucumber, hot pepper paste, crushed tomato salad, and various eggplant specialties to name a few, made for a very healthy diet. As the main course, shrimp, chicken or lamb *tavas* or casseroles, and *kebabs* rounded out a delicious meal. Two favorite restaurants Liz and I enjoyed across from the air base were the "Red Onion" and the "Moonlight Café" where we were always warmly greeted by name and one could purchase a three-course meal for less than $5.00 US.

Liz and I also spent a number of pleasurable weekends in Kiz Kalesi, a holiday resort two hours from Adana, with fine sandy beaches, inexpensive motels and hotels, outstanding seafood restaurants, bars, and campsites. A number of our educators purchased condos overlooking the majestic Mediterranean here, and a few who have since departed Turkey, come back yearly to visit their apartments. Two castles which were a part of the ancient city of Korykos make this town famous: Castle-by-the-Sea and Castle-in-the-Sea, which can be reached by swimming or boat.

Although not in the line of duty as superintendent of the Mediterranean District, in the summer of 2000, I visited the Incan ruins at Machu Picchu in Peru, my seventy-eighth country. This ancient village surrounded by the majestic, snow-covered Andes Mountains will be a scene long remembered.

There were a few downsides to life in Turkey. An earthquake in Adana killed approximately one hundred people and destroyed numerous homes while we were there. In our second to last year, Turkish workers on base went on a sixty-day strike. There was no garbage collection, so the refuse was piled high. Tires were slashed, and shards of glass were thrown onto the roads. At school, when only a bare minimum of cleaning folks reported for duty, teachers had to pitch in to clean their rooms and the toilet facilities. The stores and restaurants outside the base were shut down, and the Command closed the BX and commissary. Since no buses were available, parents had to drive their kids to school. Throughout that time, I was required to attend meetings with the Commanding Officer twice daily to assess the security situation and to map out strategies for continuing base services. To top things off, we experienced a "lock down alert" at school when word came that an Iraqi missile was heading our way. Thankfully, it turned out to be a false alarm.

Finally, during what was to be our last week in Turkey, we were in a major auto accident while driving to the beach resort of Kiz Kalezi, totaling our rental car and causing injuries to both

Liz and her friend, Faye, who was visiting us from the United States. Faye spent three weeks in a local hospital before she could be medically evacuated.

As in all organizations, the pendulum swings back and forth, and there was a move in DoDDS to consolidate the eight European Districts into five. Our school district was slated to close in June at the end of the school year 2001. I was promised a position in the reorganization.

In the spring of 2001, I received a call from European Director, Diana Ohman, assigning me as superintendent of the newly reorganized Mediterranean District with headquarters in Vicenza, Italy. The district included portions of my old territory, Spain and Turkey, plus thirteen schools in Italy—twenty-one schools in all. American military commanders in Turkey, who were concerned that they had no district representative in the reorganization, seemed pleased that I would continue as superintendent. I promised frequent visits and good oversight. I was honored when the very supportive Inçirlik Wing Commander, Col. Thomas "Rudy" Wright, hosted a Change of Command ceremony for me.

During our final Memorial Day weekend there, our knowledgeable Turkish host nation teacher at Inçirlik High, Nuran Avsar, escorted a number of us faculty and staff on a spectacular tour of eastern Turkey. We visited the Lake Von area and rode a bus along the Turkish-Iranian border to Mt. Ararat, where tradition says Noah's Ark came to rest after the Flood.

Traveling on average two out of every four weeks had been a little wearing on this old body. However, this assignment was extremely remarkable, and Liz and I made lasting friends with many of the dedicated American teachers and administrators as well as with local Turkish and Bahraini educators in the district. I cannot fail to mention five of our very loyal Turkish employees and friends at the Inçirlik schools who enriched our lives in

Turkey: Yuksel Tirang and Huseyin Eradyn at the elementary school, Tevfik Esberk and Nuran Avsar at the high school, and my faithful district secretary, Gul Inal.

[9]

Italy years 2001-2005

Our DoDDS Mediterranean Office from 2001 to 2005 was located in Vicenza, Italy, on Camp Ederle, home to the Southern European Task Force and the 173rd Airborne Brigade, the largest U.S. garrison in Europe. This centrally located Veneto Renaissance city is ideally situated an hour's drive or train ride to Verona, Padua, Venice, the Dolomites, and Treviso, while Milano, Bolzano, Bologna, and Ravenna can each be reached in a day's trip. Famous for its gold industry, Vicenza hosts the world's largest gold exhibition twice a year.

I was fortunate that Dr. Jennifer Beckwith, assistant superintendent, had served as the acting superintendent in Italy the year prior to my arrival and was knowledgeable in all aspects of the operation. Since a number of the schools in Italy were accessible by car, she took the wheel in her new Mercedes, escorting me on my initial visits. I often shaded my eyes while she negotiated the winding, curvy roads in Tuscany on the way to Livorno School or sped through the traffic at Naples toward Gaeta, not daring to watch when she raced on the *autostrade* to Verona airport, completing in thirty minutes what should have been a forty-five-minute ride.

My first flying venture with Jennifer started as a routine visit to our La Maddalena School on the island of Sardinia. On a sunny Italian morning, we drove a rental car from Vicenza to the Verona Airport where we boarded a flight to Olbia, Sardinia. In Olbia, we rented another car for the forty-five-minute drive to the town of Palau where Jennifer drove onto a ferry for the twenty-minute crossing to La Maddalena.

Nonchalantly entering our hotel, we wondered why all the guests were gathered around the lobby television set. A plane, they told us, had flown into one of the Twin Towers in New York City, and a second plane had just crashed into the other tower. The date was September 11, and America was under attack.

Fortunately, our able Chief of Staff in Vicenza, Kathy Zdanowski, handled the numerous security and coordination issues between the Washington and European headquarters and kept me informed by cell phone. Schools were closed the following day; however, Jennifer and I held a quick meeting with the commanding officer and the school principal, Barbara Mueller, before returning home via Rome.

In subsequent years, I was immeasurably impressed with the adept staff at La Maddalena and its dynamic principal, Stephanie El Sayed, providing expert service to our students in this isolated location. My visits always included evening dinners with staff members in the cozy restaurants of this quaint town on the Mediterranean.

Visiting each of my new schools in Italy was exciting. The final construction phase of a new, ultramodern K-12 school at Aviano in the north had stopped when the original contractor ran short of funds. I arrived just as work had resumed, and parents and the command urged us to open the new school at midyear. Following numerous meetings with military commanders and engineers, DoDDS project officer, Greg Page, and I finally convinced the command that the building would not be ready until the start of the following school year.

The new complex eventually emerged as a world class facility. The three able administrators, Doug McEnery at the high school, Susan Pope at the middle school, and Missy Klopfer at the elementary, worked harmoniously with their teaching staffs to offer students a superb educational program. Both Doug and Missy would receive the honor of Secondary and Elementary Principal of the Year, respectively. Doug's assistant, Susan Page, was honored as Assistant Principal of the Year. Susan Pope, working at the middle school without an assistant, ably brought her school to model status.

Another journey took me to Sicily, where we operated a K-12 school in the shadow of Mt. Etna, near the bustling city of Catania. Principal Jim Bowers drove me from the airport along winding roads lined with fragrant orange groves to the Sigonella Naval Base. Operating the school of 1200 students was a challenge, especially since many of the buildings were substandard. After I had addressed the faculty and visited classrooms, Jim and his wife, Anne, hosted me for dinner. Before my flight left on Saturday morning, they escorted me through the crowded, colorful fresh fish market in Catania. The *Pescheria*, located near Elephant Square or *Piazza Duomo,* is probably the most picturesque and typical of the Sicilian markets. To advertise, the vendor holds his hand close to his mouth and yells out the names of that day's catch. The whole scene is loud and very busy as Sicilians dispute the freshness of the fish and barter on the price.

At the conclusion of the following school year, when Jim received a promotion to our DoDEA office in Arlington, the Sigonella school was divided into separate entities—the high school administered by Marj Lewallen and the elementary school by Fran Austin. Both would spend countless hours in upgrading the curriculum and overseeing an ambitious building program.

The Verona School in northern Italy was scheduled to close in two years, but before that happened, I was fortunate to visit this excellent small school as well as this romantic town with its famous amphitheater, site of a world-renowned summer opera festival. Tim Erickson was my first administrator in Verona, followed by Essie Grant who closed the school.

Tim was promoted as principal to the school at Gaeta. This seacoast city, strategically located approximately an hour north of Naples, served as headquarters for the 6th Fleet. The admiral and the majority of Navy personnel resided onboard the Flagship, *USS La Salle*, anchored there. To reward scholastic achievement each month, honor roll students were given a tour of the flagship, and I was able to join them on a couple of visits.

The Livorno school, ably led by my longtime friend, Cathy Magni, was located near the city of Pisa and the legendary Tuscan hill towns. This high school won a number of awards for its topnotch AVID program. Small classes of only six to eight students made this an ideal school in which to teach. Cathy and her artist husband, Mimmo, both being expert chefs, treated me to numerous delicious Italian meals in their home.

The large faculty at the U.S. Navy Naples school, situated at Gricignano north of Naples, challenged my name recall ability. Fortunately, a number of teachers had worked with me in Korea. By studying the yearbook and staff photos taken by Elsa Martinez and the host nation instructor, Alfredo Criscuolo, combined with classroom visits and social events, I learned to recognize and appreciate the individual contributions of this talented staff. Kay Galloway, high school principal, was highly respected by the command and the faculty. Carol Cressey was an experienced large school elementary principal, followed later by Rich Alix, who would receive the honor of Elementary Principal of the Year. I treasure my memories of the outstanding Neapolitan cuisine, especially the delicious seafood pasta, and of excursions through the surrounding area, including a drive along the scenic Amalfi Coast with Assistant Principal Nadine Sapiente.

The district office was located adjacent to the Vicenza Schools. Parents of our students, headquartered with the 173rd Brigade at Camp Ederle, were among the first brave men and women to parachute into Iraq in 2003, and many endured subsequent tours to Iraq and Afghanistan. Teachers, counselors, psychologists, and administrators, under the able leadership of Kathy Cummings and later Kathleen Reiss at the high school and Alice Herring at the elementary school, did a yeoman's job assisting students and families with wartime deployment and grief issues by working overtime to ensure a stable environment for our students. To the credit of the faculty, test scores never suffered during these stressful times.

My district staff, supervised by Sam Menniti, Carl Albrecht, and Charlie Helmstetler, worked harmoniously with our schools. Engineers Steve Arn and Shelly Arnoldi were responsible for planning and overseeing numerous new school construction projects. Finance Chief Paul Saldano, supported by Paul Clifton, Matt Polen, and Jessie Eguia, insured timely equipment and furniture orders and paid the bills. Tim Krause, Reggie Gebo, and Alan Young were responsible for force protection. Curriculum liaisons Dana Jackson, Sadie Fairley, Gay Marek, Becky Vinson, and Rebecca Dunn supported teachers with standards-based instructional strategies and curriculum expertise. Richard Duncan, Dale Moore, and Nancy Martin provided technology expertise. The personnel staff was headed by Lynn Conklin and later Barbara Harris, while secretary Beth Mitchell had the task of ensuring that reports went out on time and of scheduling my numerous trips.

Memories of nightly and weekend strolls into the old town of Vicenza and its environs will remain with me for the rest of my life. Numerous buildings designed by the world-famous architect, Andrea Palladio, included splendid downtown churches and cathedrals as well as fabulous villas, the most famous being Palladio's La Rotonda on the eastern outskirts surrounded by vineyards. I enjoyed strolling along ancient cobblestone streets and climbing the endless steps to the magnificent Basilica Monte Berico, then pausing to gaze at the spectacular view of the city and the nearby Dolomite Mountains from the restaurant terrace opposite the basilica.

The downtown city square, Piazza Dei Signori, dominated by Palladio's Basilica, a huge medieval building, was a great place to sit with friends and colleagues in trendy outdoor restaurants and cafes, or to sample the flavor choices at *gelaterias* serving the refreshing Italian *gelato* or ice cream, based on water and fruit juices, originally brought to Sicily by the Moors from North Africa. We arranged to hold commencement exercises for Vicenza seniors within the Teatro Olimpico, the world's first indoor amphitheater, dating back to 1580, where, appropriately, the Olympic competitions in this historic landmark did not feature sports, but rather, philosophy, music, poetry, and science.

My good friend, Willi Reiss, a retired German Navy Captain and onetime skipper of the flagship *Rommel, was* my frequent walking partner and became a knowledgeable tour guide to many of our American visitors. He and I looked forward to Saturday afternoon outings in Vicenza and environs, including a stroll around the nearby Lake Fimon. Afterwards, we sat on the café terrace next to the lake, quenching our thirst with a cool beer or two.

Charlie and Linda Hofstetler, Sarah and Paul Clifton, and Sam Menniti often joined Liz and me in fabulous meals served with delicious red house wine at our favorite restaurants in the area. A particular favorite was a little pizzeria at the foot of Mount Berico, the Trattoria Venticinque Tues Mayo owned by our good friend, Nicola, where we were always welcome. He personally greeted us on each visit and served us a complementary bruschetta toast and *limoncello*, a delicious Italian liquor. Whenever he saw me descend the hill from one of my walks, he invited me in for a beer and pizza dough bread and cheese.

My final school year, 2004-2005, was a nostalgic one, especially the second semester as I bid farewell to teachers, administrators, and commanders throughout the Mediterranean District. Each school planned a special event: an evening dinner with the staff in La Maddalena, an after-school buffet in Livorno; a picnic lunch in Vicenza; a barbeque and school assembly with Steve and Cindy Hain and the staff in Sevilla; and a faculty party at the home of Alice Rambo and Steve Payne in Rota. Patty and Mike Awalt, Rich Alix, Cathy Downs, and Nadine Sapiente at Naples hosted faculty parties in their homes. In addition to official school events, Becky Vinson and Kathy Turner hosted a party at Becky's house for us and acquaintances we have known throughout our careers. Numerous teachers came, especially from Italy, Belgium, the Netherlands, Germany, and England.

The mother of all farewell functions, however, planned by Chief of Staff Carl Albrecht and Assistant Superintendent Sam Menniti, took place on May 26 in combination with our last administrators' meeting. In attendance at the fabulous hotel resort in the spa town of Abano near Venice were 150 plus guests. The grand event included a six-course dinner, speeches by various commanders, a fabulous music and dance medley led by Fran Austin and her sister administrators, fireworks, a Korean tourist group who sang *Aryang*, and dancing. It was a lifetime event that Liz and I will never forget.

After the farewells, it was back to work, especially for Liz. Packing as well as thousands of other details, to include clearing scores of U.S. post and Italian offices, were part of the final move. A short Fourth of July weekend trip to Kirchdorf, Austria, where we had spent yearly skiing trips while living in Hanau, was a welcome reprieve during that long, scorching summer.

We finally departed the Ederle Inn early on July 31, 2005 to the farewell wishes of my wonderful Mediterranean staff, boarding a bus for one last trip to the Venice airport. Forty-five years of a fabulous adventure overseas had come to a close.

Epilogue 1995-2020

After a lifetime of adventures, how could I face retirement? Liz was busy arranging furniture and unpacking 30,000 pounds of household goods in our beautiful new home near Jacksonville, Florida.

One morning shortly after retirement, I accompanied her to our local Publix supermarket. While she was shopping, I noticed a computer in the corner of the store. I filled out my resume, including various positions and advanced degrees. When the store manager interviewed me a few days later, he seemed somewhat concerned about my qualifications. I mentioned that I had grocery experience at Alberts in Cincinnati during high school. He seemed relieved and said, "you are hired." Inquiring about my position, he emphatically stated, "you are a bagger."

I loved my job and made friends with numerous customers and employees. After my third year at Publix, part time maintenance work was added to my other duties during periods when the custodian was on vacation. I started at 5 am in the morning, swept the entire store, and operated a huge electric scrubbing machine. On one of my initial attempts with the scrubber, I knocked over three store displays, leaked cleaning fluid all over the aisles, and by pushing the backup lever, pinned myself against the wall much to the consternation of the department managers. I was able to clean the mess quickly with a little help from my "friends." They all knew my name and moved quickly out of the way when they heard the scrubber approach. I continued working at Publix until May of 2019, when a hip replacement due to a fall ended my tenure.

Liz and I were able to return to both Italy and Germany before she fell ill. Tragically she died in 2017 and daughter Kathy died in Denver two years later after a long bout with PTSD.

Three years later I renewed my long-time friendship with Gladys Kuehn. I was best man in their wedding in Miles City, Montana in 1959, and her husband was my good friend in Cincinnati.

Gladys and I went on a short trip to Germany in October 2019 with the explicit purpose of continuing family research, and to revisit with good friends in Kaiserslautern, Heidelberg, Weierhof and Ruedesheim. I was anxious to share my hometown of Frankfurt with Gladys, and to introduce her to such local delicacies as hand cheese with music, herring, and blood sausage. She snubbed her nose at my selections however, she did enjoy an array of schnitzels, sausages and spaetzele. We traveled everywhere by train, whizzing by rolling hills and idyllic villages, and alongside golden vineyards which had recently been harvested.

In Frankfurt, after visiting several historic research centers, I was able to at last confirm that my grandmother and aunt were exterminated in the Lodz, Poland concentration camp. Although it was a sunny day, my head was clouded with thoughts of what they must have endured. A month after returning from Germany I received the following letter:

Dear Mr. Ellinger,

"I am writing with the hope of locating Thomas Ellinger, son of Walter Ellinger, (born 1899 in Frankfurt, Germany), the grandson of Alice Ellinger (1872, also of Frankfurt, Germany).

Alice Ellinger was a member of the Cäcilian Choir in Frankfurt. During the Nazi regime, the choir no longer allowed the Jewish members to participate, in compliance with government regulations. It saddens us that Alice and her daughter Olga were both sent to the Ghetto Lodz in Poland and died there. Alice's son Walter was released from Buchenwald, with the help of Quakers, first to England and then to America.

Last year the Cäcilian choir celebrated its 200th anniversary. This was a cause to revisit our history. In doing so, we realized how the choir acted towards its Jewish members. In some cases, it was admirable, how the relationships formed in the choir helped to protect some members. However, there was confirmation to the governing powers and our Jewish members were not allowed to sing with the choir after the regime change.

We reviewed who our Jewish members were at the time before WWII, and that a few families have not been remembered here in Frankfurt with a "Stolpenstein" in front of their residence. The plaque is to remind all walking by of those who lived in the house and how they were treated during the Nazi regime, whether they were murdered in a concentration camp, forced into committing suicide or into exile.

Our choir is planning to dedicate Stolpensteine to your father, aunt, and grandmother, to remind us of the need to stand up for justice and mercy in our daily life. As relatives, we would be honored if you would also be able to attend this ceremony in June 2020".

Sincerely
Mary Biskup

Mary's choir partner and friend, Irene Kayser provided additional information about my Dad's internment in Buchenwald as a "protected "prisoner and his subsequent release to England and the U.S.

With COVID-19, the ceremony was postponed until October 2020 and if I am not able to travel at that time, I can arrange a private ceremony at the former residences of my father and grandmother and aunt.

Receiving award from U.S. General, Gary E. Luck

North Korean soldier at Demilitarized zone

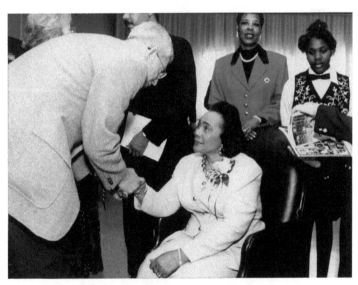

With Coretta Scott King, wife of Dr. Martin Luther King, Jr.

With Dr. Alumran, school board president, Bahrain School

Author calling a school from Cappadocia, Turkey

Seoul Tower

Index

9 781524 315764